GW01368305

FROM BELFAST

Edited by Allison Dowse

First published in Great Britain in 2000 by
YOUNG WRITERS
Remus House,
Coltsfoot Drive,
Woodston,
Peterborough, PE2 9JX
Telephone (01733) 890066

All Rights Reserved

Copyright Contributors 1999

HB ISBN 0 75431 836 2
SB ISBN 0 75431 837 0

FOREWORD

This year, the Young Writers' Future Voices competition proudly presents a showcase of the best poetic talent from over 42,000 up-and-coming writers nationwide.

Successful in continuing our aim of promoting writing and creativity in children, our regional anthologies give a vivid insight into the thoughts, emotions and experiences of today's younger generation, displaying their inventive writing in its originality.

The thought, effort, imagination and hard work put into each poem impressed us all and again the task of editing proved challenging due to the quality of entries received, but was nevertheless enjoyable. We hope you are as pleased as we are with the final selection and that you continue to enjoy *Future Voices From Belfast* for many years to come.

Contents

Ashfield Girls' High School
Paula Blair	1
Nicola Dougherty	2
Louise Boyd	2
Charlotte McLean	3
Pamela Cardy	4
Kelly Lindsay	4
Claire Bloomer	5
Julie Kerr	6
Emma Maginnis	7
Jemma Morrison	7
Julie McClean	8
Nicole Thompson	8
Catrina McIntyre	9
Sarah Close	10
Lyndsay Charlotte McAleer	10
Haley Wilson	11
Danielle Carroll	12
Katherine Ross	12
Lisa Magowan	13
Nicola Louise Livingstone	14
Hollie Baird	14
Hayley Johnston	15
Angela Jehan	16
Lindsay Morrison	16
Natasha McCready	17
Claire Montgomery	18
Cathy Lenaghan	18
Samantha Hornby	19
Rebecca Hastings	20
Stephanie Allen	20
Laura Bush	21
Kristina Watson	22
Karen Higgins	23
Fallon Carter	24
Julie Yarr	24

Jacqueline Lockhart	25
Claire McFarland	26
Cheryl Morgan	26
Jenny Pratt	27
Louise Matthews	28
Jennifer Thompson	29
Wendy Murray	30
Stacy Ward	31
Karla Tann	32
Jenna Steele	33
Lindsey Richardson	34
Christina Weaver	35
Sarah Freel	36
Stephanie Holt	37
Amy Bovis	38
Lyndsay McBride	39
Reine Watt	40
Laura Campbell	41
Joanna Hawkins	42
Lyndsey Holt	43
Julieanne Mercer	44
Deborah Trotter	45
Lesley Trotter	46
Lindsay Blair	47

Hunterhouse College

Patricia Johnston	48
Rosanna Perry	49
Suzanne Hutchison	50
Faye Gillespie	51
Louise Adair	52
Rhiannon Docherty	53
Laura Watts	54

Methodist College

James Morrow	54
Sara Malone	55
Alastair Little	56

John Russell	57
Emma Weir	58
Robert Todd	59
Sarah Martin	60
Mark Ferguson	61
Lauren Donaghy	62
Scott Thompson	63
Susannah Gleadhill	64
Hyun-Kyoung Koo	64
Louise Waugh	65
Neil Dunn	66
Carole Wilson	67
Matthew Bell	68
Laura Collins	69
Deborah Boyd	70
Andrew McIntyre	71
Matthew Crosby	72
Eleanor Gilmore	72
Victoria Mackay	73
Laura Grant	74
Steven Christie	75
Judith Pollock	76
Christopher Sanlon	77

Orangefield High School

Kris McConkey	78
Raymond Jordan	78
David Hogg	79
Susan Forsythe	80
Colin Wellington	80
Jonathan Connolly	81
Glen Blackmore	81
Steven Burns	81
Chris Murphy	82
Nikki Robinson	82
Pamela Todd	83
Mark Warren	84
Andrew Patterson	84

Pamela Connolly	85
Trudie Curran	86
Carrie Martin	86
Laura McBride	87
Louise Bell	88
Ashley McFarland	89
Louis Tittensor	89
Gemma Bowers	90
Robert Speers	90
Craig Greer	91
Marco Chambers	92
Amy King	92
David Blair	93
Alana Bell	94
Stacey Youll	94
David McConkey	95
Sarah Moore	96
Annette Girvin	96
Michelle McCausland	97
Sammy-Joe Smith	98
Mark Carson	98
Christine Andrews	99
Selene McKeown	100
Glenn Tann	100
Leanne Macey-Lillie	101
Lisa Conlane	101
Heather Gorman	102
Kirsty Davidson	102
Graham Wallace	103
Mark McConnell	103
Craig Magee	104
Darren Birch	104
Gina Kennedy	105
Danielle Dickey	106
Ashley McKay	106

Our Lady And St Patrick's College
                Chris McWilliams   107

Our Lady Of Mercy Secondary School
                Laura McCarthy   108
                Susanne Thomas   108
                Karen Jones   109
                Grace Smyth   109
                Amanda Shields   110
                Deborah Kane   110
                Aisling Taylor   111
                Emma Gibson   112
                Denise Clarken   112
                Danielle McAuley   113
                Sarah Louise Magee   113
                Mary-Beth Fennell   114
                Caoimhe O'Donnell   114
                Sarah McLarnon   115
                Martine Magee   116
                Christine Murphy   116

St Dominic's High School
                Geraldine Boyle   117
                Bernadette McQuillan   118
                Noirin Kearney   118
                Roisin McIlduff   119
                Úna Méabh Herron   120
                Katrina Brennan   121
                Pauline Gough   122
                Oonagh Barronwell   123
                Karen Molloy   124
                Paula Kearney   124
                Mary Moran   125
                Karen McIlvenny   126
                Claire Rooney   127
                Ita Monaghan   128
                Clara McCurdy   128
                Clare Galway   129

Kathy Crawford	130
Helen Brady	130
Sarah McGlinchey	131
Sorcha Eastwood	132
Siobhán Gibson	133
Roisin Walsh	133
Kathleen Healey	134
Sinéad Burns	134
Lyndsay Meredith	135
Katie McGarry	135
Sarah Mc Caul	136
Sarah O'Connell	137
Emer Denny	138
Eva Dugan	139
Bronagh Diamond	139
Clare Hilland	140
Clíodhna Massey	141

St Rose's High School

Bronagh Clarke	141
Lyndsey Murray	142
Seáneen Mallon	143
Bronagh McGlinchey	144
Colleen Brady	144
Catherine Rock	145
Joanne Donnelly	146
Denise Keatings	147
Claire Carson	148
Katrina Connolly	148
Kaleena Morelli	149
Deborah O'Neill	150
Antoinette Smith	151
Charlene Barkley	152
Yolanda Cox	153
Deirdre Melly	154
Claire Agnew	154
Louise McKenna	155
Lena Buttimer	156

Laura Osborne	156
Lindsey McVarnock	157
Lindsay Mullan	158
Ciara Leathem	158
Stephanie McCann	159
Katrina Morgan	159
Donna Marie Rock	160
Francine Milnes	160
Susanna Toner	161
Hannah Donnelly	162
Emma Brady	162
Margarette Shortt	163
Patricia Taggart	164
Aisling Kelly	164
Francine Jack	165
Claire Marie Kerr	166
Thomasina Lindsay	166
Letitia Mulgrave	167
Orlaith Malocco	167
Mairead McShane	168

Strathearn School

Gillian Armstrong	168
Helen Bell	169
Nadine Norwood	170
Ruth Osborne	170
Emma Cranstone	171
Pauline Twibill	172
Sarah McMinn	172
Andrea Leebody	173
Stephanie MacNeill	174
Vicky Bill	174
Susan Moore	175
Danielle Futter	176
Julia Bailey	176
Laura Matthews	177
Chantelle Derrick	177
Louise Rodgers	178

Nicola Keenan	178
Claire Cooper	179
Holly Martin	180
Christine Millar	180
Megan Thompson	181
Ruth Caven	181
Katherine Dalzell	182
Heather MacNeill	182
Sarah Meadows	183
Laura Nixon	184
Ruth-Anne Wilgar	184
Kathryn Duff	185
Emma Campbell	185
Jennifer Stewart	186
Katie Bill	186
Katherine Best	187
Emma Thompson	188
Emily Wyeth	188
Faye Caldwell	189
Julie Hedley	190
Elaine Clarke	190
Ashley Porter	191
Gillian Brown	192
Amy McLaughlin	192
Jennifer Cash	193
Katie Higgins	193
Gemma Scott	194
Claire Kirker	194
Rachel Manning	195
Caroline Bole	196
Florence Andrew	196
Joanne McKeown	197
Claire Thompson	198
Elizabeth Bree	199
Rachelle Thompson	200
Jacci McLellan	200
Jennylee Cooling	201
Gemma McGuire	202

Jenna Fielding	202
Rachel Grimes	203
Laura Wilson	204
Rachel Boyd	205
Jamielee Bingham	205
Rachael O'Flaherty	206

Victoria College

Wendy McCallin	206
Laura Martin	207
Christine Sterrett	208
Katie Burrell	208
Amy Phillips	209
Paula Lyons	210
Leann MaCaulay	211
Jillian Reid	212
Janine McKnight	212
Catherine Magee	213
Naomi Andrews	214
Stephney Girvan	214
Nicola Beattie	215
Cathryn Crockett	215
Kirsty Shawe	216
Rachel Johnson	217
Carla Cochrane	217
Kerry Floyd	218
Catherine Barbour	219
Helen De Ornellas	220
Christine Devenney	220
Karen Nicholl	221
Jade Adair	222
Sarah Dunlop	222
Jennine Buchanan	223

Wellington College

Keith Killops	223
Dean Johnston	224
Rachel Gough	224

Angela Shields	225
Matthew Shearer	226
Pamela Johnston	226
Ross Dunlop	227
John Mooney	228
Mark Burch	229
Matthew Cranston	230
Steven McClintock	230
Christopher Deary	231
Thomas Allison	232
Sarah Smith	233
Gillian Elder	234
Julie Anderson	234
Robert Smyth	235
Victoria McAuley	236

The Poems

MY PARADISE

My 'Paradise' is a lost and lonely place,
The streets are hard and cruel.
The suffering, the anguish, the pain and the torture
Are felt throughout the gloom.
Humans and creatures alike have all lost hope
Of happiness, their pleasures forsaken.
Life seems meaningless to those who care
For joy, their lust for life taken.
My world seemed such a happy place,
Was that just an illusion?
Now, dull appearance with atmosphere to match,
Just adds to my confusion.
I would watch them, sad, afraid and alone,
Lost souls wandering aimlessly around streets.
I wonder what would happen if
One of those, I should greet.
Would they turn and walk away?
Would they crack their face to smile in reply?
I do not know what will become of them.
Will they be this miserable 'til the day they die?

Somehow I don't fit in with this way of life
Is my love of existence my only vice?
Here life is hard and even intolerable,
But still, this is my 'Paradise'.

Paula Blair (14)
Ashfield Girls' High School

FIRE

Fire can start in any home,
One spark is all that's needed,
It's an awful thought,
A terrible sight,
I hope we never see it.

Alarms will sound, the smoke will rise,
Unable to breathe and burning eyes,
The sounds of rescue ring through the city,
Lives are lost it's an awful pity.

The fire brigade will smash down the door,
Their mission to save lives once more,
An awful job they must be brave,
For the ones that are not saved will end up in a grave.

The doctors mend the burns to the bone,
Of a little child who was left alone,
The mother thought she would not be long,
But now she knows that she was wrong.

Lessons on fire we must know,
Because to lose your home is a terrible blow,
A home burnt down can be replaced,
When lives are lost it's a terrible waste.

Nicola Dougherty (15)
Ashfield Girls' High School

PARADISE ISLAND

The ocean is deep blue, calm
Wild flowers are filled with colour.
The sun is bright and hot,
The sand golden and slightly crisp.

Water ripples down the mountainside
The sky is pale blue, almost clear.
The scents of air, so free,
Everything blends to make the perfect paradise.

Louise Boyd (14)
Ashfield Girls' High School

DEATH

When I got up one morning,
I went down to the kitchen below
To find my mother crying,
So I asked her to take it slow.

'What's wrong?' I cried
'Why do you weep?'
'It's your father' she said
She could barely stand on her feet.

'What's wrong with him,
What's happened
I want to know right now.
If he's hurt or missing or just out of town.'

'He's dead!' she cried
Someone has killed him
They sent him to heaven
When they should be in prison.

'Oh no' I cried
'It's so unfair'
He was my father
But . . . no one seems to care . . .

Charlotte McLean (14)
Ashfield Girls' High School

SOMEONE SPECIAL TO ME!

There isn't a day gone by,
When I don't think about you.
I promised myself I would not cry,
I don't know what to do.

I will always have the memories
Which I will treasure and keep
Never to be forgot
What you meant, we loved you a lot.

I am the youngest
I was the closest to you
But now you're gone
Time will have to linger on.

Seeing you there with a
Smile upon your face
Would lift me up and
Fill me with grace.

You were always someone special
Someone kind and true
You'll never be forgotten
For we thought the world of *you!*

Pamela Cardy (14)
Ashfield Girls' High School

FRIENDS

Friends are very caring
They think of you in a good way
They can sometimes be a bit annoying
Your friends would always stick up for you.

Friends are fun
Sometimes a bit noisy
Friends are very good to you
And you would be lost without them.

Kelly Lindsay (11)
Ashfield Girls' High School

PARADISE

No one to bug you
On your own all day long
Orange with an ice cube
Like a line from a song.

A white sandy beach
A deep blue ocean
Out of everyone's reach
Like I've drunk a magic potion.

Colourful birds
Big palm trees
Could not be explained in words
How pretty the sea is.

The sun is so bright
It's the most beautiful sight.
I want to stay here forever
It couldn't get any better.

It's half past eight
And it's time to go to school.
To think that it was real
I am such a fool!

Claire Bloomer (14)
Ashfield Girls' High School

SCHOOL

School is good when you're in the mood
For a hard day's work at school
Children beaming
Teachers screaming
How much can you take?

Heads exploding
Chalk eroding
Paper being thrown about
Hands being raised from us in doubt
How much can you take?

Chairs are swinging
Children singing
Noise is travelling far
Bells are sounding
Hearts are pounding
How much can you take?

Corridors are flowing
With children they are growing
You can hardly move an inch
Hair tied back
How stupid we look
How much can you take?

Julie Kerr (14)
Ashfield Girls' High School

FRIENDS

Friends are people who stick up for you,
Friends are people you tell secrets to,
Friends are people who respect you
And friends are people who understand you!

We can count on them in times of need
And they will always give advice,
Although sometimes they can be nasty,
They usually are quite nice!

Friends are great fun,
They make up your social life,
They will also guide or direct you,
Especially through times of strife!

Emma Maginnis (14)
Ashfield Girls' High School

PARADISE

I have my own little paradise and it's not far from here,
In fact it's in my head, when I think and when I dream.
I go to my little paradise, when things are getting tough,
I go when I'm feeling sad or even when I'm not.
My paradise has a beach and a jungle filled with trees,
It also has a lagoon and small coral reef.

My paradise helps me, when I'm feeling mad
And it even calms me down.
But I don't care if it's not real, because it only belongs to me
And no one has to know except for you and me.

Jemma Morrison (14)
Ashfield Girls' High School

CHRISTMAS

All the streets are humming,
With the bright lights everywhere
All the children counting,
The hours to Christmas Day.

Snow is on the treetops,
Snow is on the ground,
Snow is on the houses,
It's falling all around.

Everyone is happy,
It's that special time of year,
When Christmas parties happen,
'Cause the special date is near.

Julie McClean (14)
Ashfield Girls' High School

WAR

Man, so cruel
Disagreements
Fighting, bombs, bullets
So many killed
River flowing with the blood
Of the innocent
Broken bodies strewn around
Families heartbroken
Man, so cruel
Killed their soul.

Nicole Thompson (11)
Ashfield Girls' High School

MY PARADISE

Cooling, calming down by the sea
Scorching, burning the sun's rays on me
Palm trees are swaying in the breeze
Oh how good it feels to live life at ease
Golden sands all along the way to me
Running and leading up to meet the sea.

All colours of blue is the still water
I can feel the sun getting hotter and hotter
The island so quiet, no movement at all
It's like being in your favourite place guarded by walls.

Walking along barefoot on the shingle
Oh how it makes my limbs all tingle
Picking up shells and little pebbles too
I threw them playfully in the sea so blue
The waves are lapping like little puppy dogs
In the distance I can see developing fog.

Go to the west I call to the sea
Don't come anywhere east near me
Shimmering, shining the crystal stones glimmer below
You can see them stretching beyond the cove.

My cocktail beside me warming up fast
The little beads of condensation trickling down the glass
If this sounds inviting enough to entice
You can place yourself in my paradise.

Catrina McIntyre (15)
Ashfield Girls' High School

Paradise

Paradise, paradise how lovely that would be,
Oh sitting on a nice warm beach looking at the clean blue sea.
I would lie under the big ball of fire,
Knowing what time it was as the sun got higher and higher.

There'd be no parents to boss me around,
They couldn't even shout at me for bathing on the ground.
I could eat all day without worry of spoiling my dinner,
Or eat nothing at all and get even thinner.

I'd be so happy, happier than anything,
I'd dance and play on the beach or maybe even sing.

Then it would start to get dark and cold
And I'd wish my mum was there to hold.
I'd start to get lonely sitting on my own,
No one to find me, because my paradise is unknown.

Paradise, paradise now I can see,
It wouldn't be paradise with no one to share it with me.

Sarah Close (14)
Ashfield Girls' High School

Gone

You used to run,
Up and down your cage,
But now that is gone
Gone up with you.

You used to jump on your football
And try to run around
But now that has gone
Gone up with you.

I still have memories,
Of how you used to be,
But that has stayed with me
And not gone up with you.

Lyndsay Charlotte McAleer (11)
Ashfield Girls' High School

MY GRANDAD

He is kind, gentle and very loving
He takes me places, special places;
Where only he and I know about.

He would drive me places I want to go,
He'd be nice to my friends, who all love him as well.
We would sit up at night and drink hot chocolate
And watch TV or read a book or even do puzzles,
But that's only when I stay over.

I would visit him almost every day,
He gives me pocket money so that I can go out
At the weekends
I don't ask for it but he insists I take it.

It's just in his nature to be kind,
I know he loves me and he knows I love him,
Very much

And so that is why my grandfather is irreplaceable,
To me.

Haley Wilson (15)
Ashfield Girls' High School

DESPERATE FREEDOM!

A pool of emotions fill my stomach
Oh look what you have done
I can't speak out I weep inside
Weep for my freedom
I suffer the silence but dread the fights
That have killed the wild one in my eyes
I feel lifeless and dead
Oh when will this end
Will my freedom ever reach me in time?
My memories are shattered, the abuse is done
Should I feel guilty I'm a daughter not a son
I know there is hope but I dare not tell
No one would understand what it's like, it's *hell!*
But I still sit and wait for my freedom to come
Sorry will never do because what's done is done.

Danielle Carroll (14)
Ashfield Girls' High School

MY PARADISE

All alone on my huge island
The sky as blue as the sea
The sand too hot to walk on
I'm glad that this is me.

I run around all day
Doing whatever I want to do
Swimming, fishing, swinging through trees
Even flying with the bees.

I eat whatever I want to
Any time or any day
Berries, nuts, bananas and coconuts
In any possible way.

I wake up from my dream once more
If only that was me
I'd eat when I want, do what I want
Now that's the life for me!

Katherine Ross (15)
Ashfield Girls' High School

HALLOWE'EN

Trick or treat, trick or treat
All the children love to scream
They go round houses, looking for money
But all they get is sweets, sweets, sweets.

All teenagers enjoy fireworks
Holding them, shooting them
Up towards the moon
The sky is lit up at night
With every rocket shining so brightly.

Hallowe'en is a scary night
With children giving people a fright
You go to parties and put people in fear
Hallowe'en is the spookiest time of year.

Ghosts and goblins, skeletons too
Who knows what's waiting round the corner for you.

Lisa Magowan (14)
Ashfield Girls' High School

ANYTHING'S POSSIBLE ON ALL HALLOWS EVE

In the midst of the night you may hear a groan,
A chain clatter and clank, a scream or moan.
Little white shadows, big black shapes,
Teeth marks of animals, scabs or scrapes.

Monsters and ugliness everywhere you go,
Not real of course, just kiddies and foe.
Ghosts and ghouls, vampire bats,
Warlocks and wizards, fierce black cats.

Blood on teeth, every gross sight,
Don't sit in the dark, burn every light.
Rap! Rap! Don't open your door,
They plead and sing 'Give us candy, more! More!'

Bloodthirsty beasties they'll squeeze you dry,
Of every penny, sweet or apple pie.
They may be kiddies, young and naive,
But don't forget, anything's possible on All Hallows Eve.

Nicola Louise Livingstone (14)
Ashfield Girls' High School

THE ANIMAL'S SECRET

The secret of a polar bear
Is that it wears pink underwear
Although you cannot see it there
It's because it's hidden by its fur.

The secret of a big black cat
Is that it is so very fat
And when you see it from above
It looks like something you could love.

The secret of a long necked giraffe
Is that it is so very daft
And even though it's very tall
If it hits its head it's bound to fall.

Hollie Baird (11)
Ashfield Girls' High School

THE FIRE

As the midnight sky glowed with stars,
Wood was piled high with leaves to make a fire,
The witches came and chanted around it
And when they had finished,
It lit, as they danced beside it.

The burning leaves hissed
And the burning wood crackled
As the ghosts and ghouls screamed and laughed,
As the yellow and orange flames
Licked the starlit sky.

When the flames died down
Dracula made a red hot path
In which the devil walked down,
As bats followed him around the path,
Meandering from side to side

And when the path came to an end,
The devil jumped into the flame,
Dragging every witch and evil thing with him,
Leaving the earth behind.

Hayley Johnston (14)
Ashfield Girls' High School

THE MILKMAN

Ernie is our milkman
I hope he's quiet for a change,
He comes so very early
The noises he makes are strange.

Now that it is autumn
He creeps in when it's dark,
The cats are all miaowing
He must get up with the lark.

I think I'll turn back over
And try to get more rest,
For if I'm tired in school
I cannot do my best.

So please Mr Ernie
Creep in nice and slow,
No rattles, shakes or bangs
And keep it nice and low.

So congratulations Ernie
You've really tried your best,
I didn't hear a thing last night
While snoring in my nest.

Angela Jehan (11)
Ashfield Girls' High School

UNTITLED

Close your eyes, who do you see?
I see you, do you see me?
Not only in my eyes, my heart too
Also in everything I say and do.

You seem to cause me so much pain
But, when I see your smile I melt again.
I feel used and you don't seem to care
Yet if you ever need me, I'll always be there.

Lindsay Morrison (16)
Ashfield Girls' High School

MOONLIGHT FRIENDS

Every night the moon shines so bright
I wonder how and when it was built,
The moon carries the sky on its shoulders,
Some nights the clouds hide it
As though the moon and I were playing a game,
A game of hide and seek
And it was winning
And the moon is at its best when full
People tell the moon their secrets
And the moon tells me
I have got a few secrets of my own
But the moon shall not tell, for it loves me and I love he
On some nights it is really special
On the nights when my friend is full
I can see witches dancing under the full moon
And on the most special night of all there is a feast
On the mountain top for all
Now you know I have one special friend, the moon
The moon is my moonlight friend
It tells me its most valuable secrets
A circle round it means trouble for me!

Natasha McCready (11)
Ashfield Girls' High School

WALKING HOME

Walking home on the dull, dark nights,
With the howling trees, falling over your steps,
With twigs that look like skeletons' bones
Rolling in the moonlight.
As the leaves fall to the ground
They seem to shrivel and curl.
They look up at me and I walk further down the road.

As I walk the radiant beams from the moon
Seem to light up my path.
Not far to go,
Just another street or two.
The walls of the lonely houses
Make my forehead drip with fear.
Then I start to run,
Run as fast as I can
And before I know it
I am home, safe and dry
Or am I?

Claire Montgomery (11)
Ashfield Girls' High School

THE FIRST BULLY

As I walked down the corridor there stood my fear
There she stood, big, evil and ready to fight
I grabbed my confidence and walked towards her
She was the tiger and I was the helpless rabbit.

There was no escape, she had seen me now
Just then she walked towards me
I felt sick, worried and scared
It was up to me to face the tiger once and for all.

She was six inches away now so no going back
She lifted her fist so tight, she made ring marks on her fingers
I knew that the next place that would be was in my face
But I couldn't let that happen.

So I grabbed her fist and threw it back
'Stop!' I shouted 'Stop it now! Leave me alone'
And that was the end of the first bully.

Cathy Lenaghan (12)
Ashfield Girls' High School

WINTER

It's the time of year when the trees are bare
It's cold outside and there is a chill in the air
There is frost on the grass and on the ground
It's on the leaves, the trees and all around
Snowflakes fall softly down
And melt on the path without a sound
From inside my house I hear the rain
Splashing against the windowpane
Nobody outside walking their dog
They're staying inside away from the fog
People go out wrapped up all warm
In case there is a terrible storm
Icicles shimmering in the sunlight
Reflecting the moonlight and stars at night
It's the time of year when we want to be
In front of the fire all warm and cosy.

Samantha Hornby (12)
Ashfield Girls' High School

Why?

Explosions and gunshots echo for miles around
Children wandering the streets alone and bewildered
Their parents and families dead.

'Why?' is asked throughout, more blasts and gunshots heard.
So much more grieving and desperation now created.

They spare no thought for the ones they hurt
Ethnic cleansing is what it's called
Thousands killed in a war of religion
It isn't humane
So why does it happen?

Rebecca Hastings (15)
Ashfield Girls' High School

Winter Trees

Swaying calmly in the winter snow
Hanging slightly above the snowy ground
Drooping wearily on its own
Rustling were the crispy leaves
Crunching were the dead, dead leaves
On the white snow blanket
Rustling were the crunchy leaves
Crackling madly were the branches
Howling spookily was the winter breeze.

Stephanie Allen (12)
Ashfield Girls' High School

CATS CRAZY

Cats are my favourite pet,
They're so cute and cuddly,
I've a cat of my own,
She's black and white
And her name is Bonnie.

Cats can either be lazy or energetic,
Some lie about,
Some even play
And some can just be crazy.

Cats are not like dogs,
They don't go for walks,
They wander around by themselves
And usually don't like being found.

Most of my family have cats,
Their names, Rascal, Charlie, Smokey
And Mr O'Malley.
They're also cute and cuddly,
I love them so much.

I'd like to have lots of cats,
Playful ones, fluffy ones, fat ones
And thin ones.
Despite their size they're all so cute
And that's why they're my favourite pet.

Laura Bush (12)
Ashfield Girls' High School

The Man Who Lives Across The Street

The man who lives across the street,
Is very spooky indeed.
I know, I know him from somewhere,
But I don't know who he is.
Who is this man
That lives across the street?

The man who lives across the street,
Can be very quiet.
His house is surrounded with quietness,
You would think nobody lives there.
I wonder who this man is
That lives across the street?

The man who lives across the street,
Has never shown his face.
He always wears a black hat
Which leans over his face.
Oh my gosh! The man is hugging that man!
He's not a man! He's a woman!
The woman who lives across the street
Is my teacher!

Kristina Watson (11)
Ashfield Girls' High School

Autumn

When autumn time comes
And the leaves begin to fall,
The nights begin to shorten
And it's not too bright at all.

The summer flowers begin to die,
They wilt and fade away,
The grass no longer needs a cut,
Not for many a day.

The days are cooler
And it's time for woolly clothes,
Put away the summer things,
We'll not be needing those.

The clocks go back an hour,
At least we get a rest,
That will give us plenty of time,
To look out our thermal vest.

Well summertime seems far away
And winter very near,
The spring seems just as far away,
But autumn is definitely here.

Karen Higgins (12)
Ashfield Girls' High School

I Am

I am a funky football fanatic.
I wonder if I will get around the world?
I hear voices chanting at a live game,
I see myself on top of the world.
I want to experience the atmosphere of a live game,
I am a funky football fanatic.

I pretend that everything is fine, when it is not!
I feel the passion of the world supporters.
I touch the sky when the ball hits the net.
I worry when we don't score,
When we're running out of time.
I cry when the game's over and everyone's gone,
I am a funky football fanatic.

I understand when things don't go my way,
I say it doesn't matter. We have next season.
I dream of seeing my team play,
I try to make everyone happy.
I hope that we'll win the Champions' League,
I am a funky football fanatic.

Fallon Carter (15)
Ashfield Girls' High School

Love

Love is like a red red rose
Touched for the very first time
My love would never die
Without you is without air.

I feel my breath shortening
Each day we float further away
I can't live without air
Please give me back my air.

I breathe no more
You gave our air away
I look at death
Without air, I have no meaning.

Julie Yarr (16)
Ashfield Girls' High School

I AM

I am a cheeky girl who laughs all the time.
I wonder when the world will end,
I hear voices deep within my mind,
I see strange things whenever I dream,
I want to become a millionaire.
I am a cheeky girl who laughs all the time.

I pretend to be a football manager and boss people about,
I feel embarrassed when people laugh at me,
I touch my silky soft skin when I am sleeping,
I worry when people become ill,
I cry when I hear that someone has died.
I am a cheeky girl who laughs all the time.

I understand that life comes to a halt,
I say life should be lived to the full,
I dream about travelling the world,
I try to do well at school.
I hope my life will be successful and long.
I am a cheeky girl who laughs all the time.

Jacqueline Lockhart (15)
Ashfield Girls' High School

I AM

I am a kind girl who likes children
I wonder what the future will hold for me
I hear strange voices deep within my mind.
I see myself as an old woman in years to come
I want to be a millionaire
I am a kind girl who likes children.

I pretend to be famous and dance in my room
I feel embarrassed if someone laughs at me.
I touch my cat's soft fur
I worry what people think of me
I cry if I see someone getting hurt
I am a kind girl who likes children.

I understand that life is short
I say live life the best you can.
I dream one day that the world will find peace
I try to help by doing whatever I can
I hope one day that my dreams will come true
I am a kind girl who likes children.

Claire McFarland (16)
Ashfield Girls' High School

DREAMS

Dreams, dreams,
What becomes of these tiny little thoughts
Shattered by the sun
Of the mystical land which I visited last night
And the spiralling sensation of flying like a kite.

The tiny mythical bubbles of the pleasant times I've spent
Searching for my time-lost hero in a three dimensional sense
Each floating little bubble showing me where my future goes
Of my hero's strength and all his fighting foes.

I heard his battle cry in the shadows of the darkness
I've seen his pain and anguish in knowing his right to die
I see him float up through the sky
To my hero's eternal heaven nearby.

Not knowing myself will I see him again
On the right path to heaven, through his strength I gain
Not knowing what my dreams will become
Of these tiny little thoughts shattered by the sun.

Cheryl Morgan (15)
Ashfield Girls' High School

I AM

I am a carefree girl who loves to shop
I wonder what the future holds for me?
I hear the sounds of my mother saying, 'You'd better do well at school'
I see me when I am older
I want to go to America and shop all day
I am a carefree girl who loves to shop.

I pretend to be a singer
I feel the sun shining down on me
I worry about my family
I cry when someone dies in my family
I am a carefree girl who loves to shop.

I understand when my friends are in trouble
I say that I am going to do well
I dreamt that I met Steve from Boyzone
I try hard in school
I hope to get a job when I leave school
I am a carefree girl who loves to shop.

Jenny Pratt (15)
Ashfield Girls' High School

I AM

I am a disco diva with a lot of ambitions
I wonder if God was just like me
I hear the screams of faithful fans at a pop concert
I see me dressed in the uniform of my ideal job
I want to live my life to the full
I am a disco diva with a lot of ambitions.

I pretend to be my favourite singer in front of my mirror
I feel like I want to scream out loud and tell my enemies
What I really think of them
I touch the soft, smooth skin of a newborn baby
I worry that my life is going to end before I have
Fulfilled my dreams
I cry at my all time classic love stories
I am a disco diva with a lot of ambitions.

I understand that someday the world will end
I say that the world will be in peace
Sometime in the future
I dream of being an actress in a Steven Speilberg movie
I try to do something worthwhile every day
I hope to lead a successful life
I am a disco diva with a lot of ambitions.

Louise Matthews (15)
Ashfield Girls' High School

I AM

I am a girl full of wonders.
I wonder what each day will bring, surprises, happiness
or sadness?
I enjoy life with all my friends and family for whom I care
for so much
I understand we are all going to die someday,
we could be young or old
I believe you have to make the most of life
as you only get one chance
I am a girl full of wonders.

I pretend I can do things that are not possible
I dream about things which could happen but I know never will
I hope I will live a long and happy life to fulfil all my dreams
I like to act out some of my dreams in front of the mirror
I want to do a lot of things that I want to do
but know I never will
I am a girl full of wonders.

I am sometimes mad when I do stupid things
I am sometimes happy when I do good things
I want to travel but wonder if I ever will
I wonder what it would be like to be on the beach
in a hot country
I wonder if I will ever get what I want in life?
I am a girl full of wonders.

Jennifer Thompson (15)
Ashfield Girls' High School

I AM

I am a typical teenager, who wants to conquer the world!
I wonder what tomorrow will bring or if I will be here to tell the tale.
I hear the screams of many fans as I will be their superstar.
I see the day when I am given gold for being an Olympic showjumper.
I want to gallop over sandy shores with sea spraying in my face.
I am a typical teenager, who wants to conquer the world!

I pretend to be a movie star, quoting lines from my favourite films.
I feel the world closing in around me.
I touch the sky with every dream I have.
I worry that someday my loved ones will die.
I cry when I am hurt.
I am a typical teenager, who wants to conquer the world!

I understand all good things must come to an end.
I say live life to the full.
I dream I will succeed in every way.
I try to be friendly to all new people I meet.
I hope the world will have eternal peace.
I am a typical teenager, who wants to conquer the world!

Wendy Murray (15)
Ashfield Girls' High School

I AM

I am an active girl who loves football
I wonder if I'll ever be a famous footballer?
I hear people stamping their feet and chanting my name,
I see the ball in front of me, the keeper in the nets,
I want to score a goal and everyone will cheer,
I am an active girl who loves football.

I pretend to take the last penalty in a cup match,
I feel everyone's eyes on me,
I touch the ball and it starts to fly,
I worry that my team won't win,
I cry if we don't,
I am an active girl who loves football.

I understand things may not last,
I say it's best to try,
I dream someday I'll touch the sky,
I try my best to do all I can,
I hope I can live my life to the full,
I am an active girl who loves football.

Stacy Ward (15)
Ashfield Girls' High School

I AM

I am a bubbly girl who loves dolphins
I wonder if pigs can fly
I hear the echoes of dolphins all around
I see one million pounds stacked up in my room
I want to be a millionaire
I am a bubbly girl who loves dolphins.

I pretend that every day is a good day
I feel like everyone is staring at me
I touch the sky but can't quite make it
I worry about my family and friends
I cry when someone close to me gets hurt
I am a bubbly girl who loves dolphins.

I understand that I will die someday
I say that I can achieve anything I want
I dream about living somewhere exotic
I try to do my best at all times
I hope that one day I can swim with the dolphins
I am a bubbly girl who loves dolphins.

Karla Tann (16)
Ashfield Girls' High School

I AM

I am a shy girl with lots of ambitions.
I wonder will I ever get married?
I hear the screaming of my young children,
I see myself in years to come as an old age pensioner.
I want to be famous.
I am a shy girl with lots of ambitions.

I pretend that I am a millionaire.
I feel all the money weighing me down,
I touch all the clothes that I want to buy,
I worry about my future life,
I cry when everything goes wrong.
I am a shy girl with lots of ambitions.

I understand that I will most likely not be famous.
I say that I am full of great intentions,
I dream of what the future holds for me,
I try to do my best in everything,
I hope that I have a good future ahead of me.
I am a shy girl with lots of ambitions.

Jenna Steele (15)
Ashfield Girls' High School

I Am

I am a caring person who wants peace in Northern Ireland.
I wonder if we will ever be able to live as friends,
I hear guns and bombs all around me,
I see people fleeing their homes in terror.
I want everyone to live as friends.
I am a caring person who wants peace in Northern Ireland.

I pretend I can make a difference,
I feel people would prefer violence.
I touch a young child's tearful face,
I worry they will grow up with this fighting.
I cry when I think of the thousands who've died.
I am a caring person who wants peace in Northern Ireland.

I understand it may take time,
I say it would work if we all made an effort.
I dream that one day it will all be over,
I try to believe someone can change it.
I hope that someone can make my dreams come true.
I am a caring person who wants peace in Northern Ireland.

Lindsey Richardson (15)
Ashfield Girls' High School

I Am

I am a very active girl who likes swimming.
I wonder how much longer my grandad will live for?
I hear my mum talking to people about me.
I see how good my stepdad is with his children,
I want to see my dad more than I do.
I am a very active girl who likes swimming.

I pretend to talk to people when I am scared,
I feel good when I have money in my hand.
I touch my face when I wash every morning,
I worry when I am sad.
I am a very active girl who likes swimming.

I understand when people fight I just get out of the way.
I say that I should get to know my stepdad better.
I dream about a boy - not just any boy but the boy I love,
The one for me, will never be.
I try to be kind to my friends and make them laugh
But if they don't like me the way I am then they are not true friends.
I hope for love, but most of all I hope for health.
I am a very active girl who likes swimming.

Christina Weaver (15)
Ashfield Girls' High School

I AM

I am a nutty girl who lives life to the full.
I wonder if I'll be a success when I'm older?
I hear my name being mentioned on the news
I see it being written beside an OBE.
I want this to happen, but it's just a dream
I am a nutty girl who lives life to the full.

I pretend I'm a stunt girl bungee jumping off bridges
I feel the cool breeze blowing in through my hair
I touch the clouds, which are smooth and soft
I worry if I'll do this, I hope that I will
I cry when I think I won't be a success
I am a nutty girl who lives life to the full.

I understand that I'll get old
I say that's life, everyone does
I dream I'll be successful and have a good job
I try my best to make people happy
I hope they're pleased and are happy for me
I am a nutty girl who lives life to the full.

Sarah Freel (15)
Ashfield Girls' High School

I Am

I am a friendly young girl with a lot of good chums
I wonder if I'll turn out just like my mum?
I hear her calling 'Get out of bed!'
I see her standing there, shaking her head
I want to have hair just like my mum's
I am a friendly young girl with a lot of good chums.

I pretend I can't hear her calling to me
I feel a sigh of relief as she goes to wake my brother, Lee
I touch the switch, the light goes off and Mum comes in mad
I worry in case she goes and tells Dad
I cry when they shout, both Dad and Mum
I am a friendly young girl with a lot of good chums.

I understand school starts in half an hour
I say, don't worry, I'll go in the car
I dream I could sleep just five minutes more
I try to make it out the bedroom door
I hope, at school there'll be no sums
I am a friendly young girl with a lot of good chums.

Stephanie Holt (15)
Ashfield Girls' High School

I Am

I am a pessimistic girl with *my own* sense and style!
I wonder will I achieve all my goals in life?
Before it's too late and I die.
I hear voices in my head whenever I'm alone and scared.
I see minds split into two and demolition destroying the Earth.
I want to be famous, to be of importance to the world.
I am a pessimistic girl with *my own* sense and style!

I pretend by putting on a brave, happy face when inside I'm crying.
I feel dragged to the four corners of the world
When life is going bad.
I touch people's hearts with hope - well I can always dream can't I?
I worry about growing old as a spinster and to have no one around me.
I cry when I'm under pressure and time is slipping away.
I am a pessimistic girl with *my own* sense and style!

I understand I can only do my best, what more can people expect?
I say 'Smile!' it can make all the difference when you feel down.
I dream of the destruction of pain and sadness so we can all be happy.
I try to feel better about myself, although it may seem impossible.
I hope to change the way society lives,
To be under the influence of *their own* minds.
I am a pessimistic girl with *my own* sense and style!

Amy Bovis (16)
Ashfield Girls' High School

I AM

I am a nutter who talks too much
I wonder what life will be like in years to come
I hear an audience cheering me on
I see their smiling faces
I want to visit the Big Apple
I am a nutter who talks too much.

I pretend to be a dancer on Top of the Pops
I feel the beat of the music
I touch the pop stars' clothes and hair
I worry that I will upset my mum
I cry when I see someone close to me crying
I am a nutter who talks too much.

I understand that one day my parents won't be there
I say everyone should be treated equally
I dream about being famous
I try to keep everyone I love happy
I hope to live life to the max
I am a nutter who talks too much.

Lyndsay McBride (16)
Ashfield Girls' High School

I Am

I am a groovy chick who likes to party.
I wonder what I will become?
I hear the screams of people enjoying themselves.
I see before me, my friends having fun.
I want to be happy throughout my life.
I am a groovy chick who likes to party.

I pretend to be happy, whenever I am not.
I feel the rhythm of music, tensing up my body.
I touch his soft, pure, carefree face.
I worry that worrying is not always the answer.
I cry when I realise that I may never see him again.
I am a groovy chick who likes to party.

I understand that all good things must come to an end.
I say how I feel, when I feel it.
I dream of being happy throughout my life.
I try to achieve my goals and ambitions that I set for myself.
I hope that we will always be together, forever.
I am a groovy chick who likes to party.

Reine Watt (15)
Ashfield Girls' High School

I AM

I am a shopaholic who loves to party.
I wonder if I'll live a full and happy life?
I hear my children saying, 'Mummy.'
I see myself in years to come with a perfect husband.
I want the experience of travelling around the world.
I am a shopaholic who loves to party.

I pretend I am a famous actress.
I feel the world is my oyster, I can do anything!
I touch Versace's spirit as I gaze longingly through his window.
I worry about the political disagreement my country is in.
I cry when I think about a member of my family dying.
I am a shopaholic who loves to party.

I understand that getting an education will help me in later life.
I say you can achieve anything if you put your mind to it.
I dream about being a millionaire and having lots of money
To spend on clothes.
I try to get along with my siblings.
I hope that I will win the lottery one day.
I am a shopaholic who loves to party.

Laura Campbell (15)
Ashfield Girls' High School

I AM

I am crazy, football crazy.
I wonder if everybody was football crazy what the world would be like?
I hear the thumps of hearts when a shot comes too close.
I see the passion in everyone's veins.
I want to experience the adrenaline all over the world.
I am crazy, football crazy.

I pretend the glory has come over and over so when it does come,
I'll know how to react.
I feel the touch of magic that greets every game.
I touch my lucky charm that has brought so much luck.
I worry that one day this passion will leave
But deep in my heart I know it never will.
I cry at the thought of David Beckham being sent off for a foul
Which *wasn't* his fault.
I am crazy, football crazy.

I understand every single person in the stadium
(Except for the rival fans of course!)
I say the chants at every game to make the little voice inside me heard.
I dream for the people to take the violence out of the game.
I try to understand both sides of the game
When a referee makes a really, really *bad* decision.
I hope to spread this happiness to my children,
The children after that and the children after that
So they can all feel this delicious pleasure
for:
I am crazy, football crazy.

Joanna Hawkins (16)
Ashfield Girls' High School

I Am

I am a crazy girl who likes to have fun
I wonder what the world has in store for me?
I hear voices in my head when I'm on my own
I see shadows follow me as I walk
I want a groovy black Corsa
I am a crazy girl who likes to have fun.

I pretend that I am racing down the motorway in my car
I feel the wind in my face as I drive
I touch the sky when I lean out my window
I worry that I won't always be crazy
I cry when I see a crashed up Corsa
I am a crazy girl who likes to have fun.

I understand that life isn't always fun
I think that we should have our say
I dream of the day I get my black Corsa
I try to have lots of fun
I hope that I will always be mad
I am a crazy girl who likes to have fun.

Lyndsey Holt (15)
Ashfield Girls' High School

I Am

I am a funky girl who loves to listen to music.
I wonder if we will ever be allowed to wear tracksuits to school?
I see the children running around the playground
shouting and playing all their fun games.
I want to do all the same things as the other children on the
playground.

I am a person who loves to hear the birds singing in the daytime.
I pretend there are bright colours around me.
I feel there is a singer coming to sing for my school.
I touch the golden leaves and I crush them up in my hands.
I worry about the trees and the wildlife.
I cry when someone hurts me a lot.

I am a funky girl who loves to listen to music.
I understand I could not become a singer.
I say let the singers sing what they really want.
I dream that I will wake up one day and all the singers will
be by my bedside.
I try my best to help old people.
I hope to hear the wind around me.
I am a funky girl who loves to listen to music.

Julieanne Mercer (16)
Ashfield Girls' High School

I AM

I am an inquisitive girl who loves to have money
I wonder if I will ever win the lottery?
I hear coins clattering together in my pocket
I see money signs in the sky
I want loads of money in my pocket
I am an inquisitive girl who loves to have money.

I pretend that I am daft but I know that I am not
I feel as if people are talking about me which upsets me
I touch the freshly washed quilt cover and enjoy the smell
I worry about the health of my father
I cry when my mother and father have arguments
I am an inquisitive girl who loves to have money.

I understand that I'm going to have to make my own decisions in life
I say that the world will never end
I dream of being successful in the future
I try to make a good impression on other people
I hope in the future I will have a good life
I am an inquisitive girl who loves to have money.

Deborah Trotter (16)
Ashfield Girls' High School

I AM

I am a fun-loving girl who loves socialising.
I wonder if I will have any children?
I hear the bell ring to tell me it's home time.
I see this world never-ending.
I want to see the poor children happy.
I am a fun-loving girl who loves socialising.

I pretend everything is alright when it's not.
I feel the world around me.
I touch the hands of those sick children.
I worry about my friends when they are sad.
I cry when I have been hurt or let down.
I am a fun-loving girl who loves socialising.

I understand I need to improve my school subjects.
I say some things I don't always mean.
I dream that one day I'll get married and have children.

I try really hard to do well at school.
I hope that I will pass most of my exams.
I am a fun-loving girl who loves socialising.

Lesley Trotter (16)
Ashfield Girls' High School

I AM

I am a fun-loving girl who loves shopping and partying.
I wonder if I will get a well paid job so I can go shopping?
I hear birds sing as I awake in the morning.
I see myself with lots of shopping bags.
I want to live in a country with many different shops.
I am a fun-loving girl who loves shopping and partying.

I pretend that money grows on trees.
I feel that shopping can help me forget my troubles.
I touch the clothes that I hope to wear.
I worry that my tree will run out of money.
I cry when I can't get out to party.
I am a fun-loving girl who loves shopping and partying.

I understand I can't shop and pay forever.
I say that I should shop until I drop.
I dream that I will shop and party forever.
I will try to get a good job
So that I can afford all the good things in life.
I hope I will be a success in whatever I do.
I am a fun-loving girl who loves shopping and partying.

Lindsay Blair (16)
Ashfield Girls' High School

LITTLE MARKY STEVENS

Little Marky Stevens sits on the wall
Nobody bothers him, nobody at all.

He sits on the corner of Batenberg Street
With his book in his hand, polished shoes on his feet.

Little Marky Stevens sits on the wall
Nobody bothers him, nobody at all!

He doesn't go to football and never wants to play
He goes to some big posh school, but doesn't have to pay!

Little Marky Stevens sits on the wall
Nobody bothers him, nobody at all!

He sits in navy blazer, bright white shirt and stripy tie,
He disagrees with fighting and vandalism, why?

Little Marky Stevens sits on the wall
Nobody bothers him, nobody at all!

He has no friends, by himself all day,
He just sits on the wall and there he'll stay!

Little Marky Stevens sits on the wall
Nobody bothers him, nobody at all!

Patricia Johnston (15)
Hunterhouse College

FRIEND

I remember that day,
The knock on the door.
'I've been phoning for days
Where were you before?'
'I've been out with a friend.
What's the matter, what's wrong?'
Silence.
'Well, it's Damien, he's dead,
He's gone -'
Silence - it's not believable,
Now the clichés start to come.
'Got his whole life ahead of him'
'He was so very young.'
Now come the stories and rumours
Of what the family's going through.
Stay quiet or send condolences?
I don't know what I should do?
I'd known him since childhood,
He'd played on my climbing frame.
Now only a handful of memories
To put to the name.
These memories remain in my mind
To keep him always alive
And now I write this poem
So his spirit will survive.

Rosanna Perry (15)
Hunterhouse College

DEEP, DARK CUPBOARD

Down in the deep, dark cupboard, dragons,
Down in the deep, dark cupboard, ghosts and ghouls.
Down in the deep, dark cupboard, bad things.
Will it always be deep and dark down there?

I hate monsters, I hate mice, take this advice!
Look carefully, they creep around, never make a sound.
I know they are there, soon you will too.
Down in the deep, dark cupboard.

Drip, drip, goes the rain, driving me insane.
The rain makes me think about what's in there.
Down in the deep, dark cupboard, scary
Think of all the spider monsters.

I never go into the deep, dark cupboard,
I've looked into it once, dark and gloomy.
Drippy and dreary, wet and stinky
Down in the deep, dark cupboard.

It's a shadow cupboard, shadows live there,
All day and all night they stay there,
In the deep, dark cupboard.
Dark, dark, dark, dark, dark, dark, shadows.

Suzanne Hutchison (14)
Hunterhouse College

Shadows

Can you hear the shadows lurking in the dark?
Watching every step you take.
Are they coming from outside?
Go on, step outside.
You're stepping into the cold, icy world.
See the trees,
See their arms, stretching out for help,
Crying, screaming in the wind and rain.
Step quickly inside
Feel the warmth, the comfort, your own.
Fast, lock the door
Deep breath
Now, look behind you
Still your sixth sense is disturbed
Making you aware of eyes upon you.
Cold shivers down your spine
Heart beating faster.
Look over to the dark corner
Can you see anything?
It's only shadows you tell yourself!
Now, start to question your thoughts,
Shadows? Shadows of who? Shadows of what?
They're moving . . .
Suddenly . . .

Faye Gillespie (16)
Hunterhouse College

MY ESCAPE

I'm alone, in the dark, in my paradise again.
My head is stinging, spinning, throbbing,
blood is gushing from my head.
I'm lapsing in and out, in and out of consciousness.
Pain is penetrating through my body.
I am alone - dumped in the cold cupboard under the stairs
My sanctuary of happiness, of all tranquillity,
peace - my escape from the wicked world.
The door is my friend, the best one.
The only one, I've ever had.
My protection, my shield, it will keep me safe.
As I clutch my knees, I rock from side to side,
to the rhythm of my pounding heart.
I smell the terror in my own breath,
my wide eyes fixed on the door to the outside world.
The stench of blood fills the air,
reminders of when I was evil.
I ruined their life,
I destroyed their happiness - their reason to live.
I'm a nobody.
A vile, cursed wretch, I'd hear her scream.
Dammed for life, the Devil's child.
'I wish you were dead!' are Mum's stinging words.
Maybe death is lonely and unloved,
Hated and rejected, just like me.
My eyelids are getting heavy,
death is drawing nearer.
I'm not afraid any more, for
death is at my door,
to assassinate my pain.

Louise Adair (14)
Hunterhouse College

THE DREAM

When we are little, we don't like the dark. The dark
means we can't see everything like the monsters lurking
in the shadows. Then when we close our eyes, we
still see darkness when in that frame of mind. So the
problem occurs again of not knowing what's out there
and maybe this is why we have nightmares.

We're all sitting in the room, waiting
Huddled up together, scared stiff while we're waiting.
Then we heard a sound, the signal
A rattle, scream, bang, it's there.
We're scared 'cause we're not waiting,
For the thing that we were awaiting, we're not waiting anymore.
It's lurking and it's knocking, luring us
We don't go to the door where it's standing, waiting
Now we're shrieking and we're screaming cause it's going
It's going to get me and all the rest of us
All for us together, waiting forever.

Rhiannon Docherty (14)
Hunterhouse College

A Feather Of Your Good Intentions

You loved me at first sight,
Purely, honestly,
With all your heart.
You loved me.

You looked past my faults
To see the beauty inside.
The only one who saw perfection,
You loved me.

I complained,
Provoked your anger,
But still I know
You loved me.

Seventeen years
And you're still here,
I know myself because
You love me.

Laura Watts (17)
Hunterhouse College

Parents

They boss you around day and night
Saying it's for your own good.
Don't say anything wrong or else
You'll put them in a bad mood.

You can't make any medical decisions
Until you're sweet sixteen
So your father is basically your king.

They pick you up from parties
They make you go to your granny's for lunch
But what you never seem to say to them
Is that they embarrass you so much.

OK so you're sweet sixteen now
And you're holding your head high in the air
Until your mother tells your new girlfriend about
You as a baby
Then you drop your head in despair.

James Morrow (14)
Methodist College

CALIBAN

Trees grow up, tall and green,
The beach is sandy, the sea is blue,
Leaves tremble in the breeze,
And spirits caper, happy and gay.

A shadow lurches across the ground,
There is a sniffing, grunting noise,
A bush is pushed aside,
Out crawls a monster, foul smelling and evil.

Caliban reaches and breaks off a branch.
He hoists it up, and the search continues,
Crouching, shuffling, watchful and wary.
Wood slung over his shoulder.

The poor, misshapen creature crawls,
Back twisted, arms bent.
So evil, and yet, so innocent.
He's never learnt right or wrong.

Sara Malone (13)
Methodist College

THE DAY I WENT INTO SPACE

Today is my very first day! The day I'll go into space!
Out of that bed. Open those windows.
See the ships of all sizes and shapes.
Vibrant, extravagant colours!
Close those windows, into my suit,
Ready and off I go!

At ship number twelve, float through the hatch.
Inside are aliens! Furry and hairy!
Others with bright, green skin.
Off to the bridge now, meet the Captain.
I am so nervous, though he is impervious!
And gives me a pleasant 'Good day.'

The Captain, nice man, I sit in his chair.
Able to see all round from this lair.
The engines gazoom. We're off that *that* tune . . .
I'm hungry now, some food to eat?
What will it be today?
Tarquillian stew? Ractorian mousse?
Just give me what's on the tray!

We're to visit planet Venix,
(a very unusual name).
There they're all clever - rumoured living forever!
Have spring sprong tresses and wear bright red dresses
daily, and in their sleep!
The engines gazoom. We land with *that* tune.

The planet floor is soft and billowy
Flowers wild and wondrously swirlery
A gentle breeze begins to dander, smelling of basil and coriander.
I begin to drift. My feet leave the ground!
Cradled by the breeze. Then pulled towards a frieze!
Will I be found? Oh yes please!

A light hand grasps my collar, the Captain begins to holler
'All aboard to return, follow me.'
I slump in my seat, too exhausted to eat.
The aliens around me now seem friendly and crown me
with a circle of green, furry hair.
The engines gazoom. We land with *that* tune . . .
Today was my very first day. The day I went into Space!

Alastair Little (13)
Methodist College

A COMMENT

A trivial comment
Picked up,
Manipulated,
Twisted out of proportion;
The sea,
Frothing red
Boils up . . .
Words tossed as spears
Barbed with jagged hooks of resentment
Lodge in mind
To be used as ammunition at a later time.

In the sea of anger,
Thoughts and resolutions sink,
Foam-flecked cascading waves
Engulf and corrode reason.
Understanding, love
Eroded by another argument.

John Russell (14)
Methodist College

A Poem On Caliban

Enchanting, but pretty.
There is excitement, but peace.
Survivors are dreaming, lost in their sleep.

A king's evil brother, a jester and Duke.
Also a ruler, a magician and enchanter watching it all.
He is casting the spells and has created the tempest.

His daughter Miranda, is in love with another,
Ferdinard must fight for her to show his love to her father.

Ariel is the beautiful spirit at hand,
Listens and watches, obeys all commands.
His tranquil music can send some to sleep.

Unlike Caliban, he has beauty and grace,
A light, glittered body and an innocent face.

Caliban is evil. Black and grey.
He is smelly and stupid and works all day.
He is beastly and sinister but cowers from fear.
He is dirty, arrogant, repulsive but weak,
Easily influenced but still fierce.

But still he appreciates the beauty of the isle,
The music and flowers that surround him.
Colours and magic are what he sees.

Caliban does not know the difference between right or wrong,
It's not his fault but he still may be blamed.
Sycorax, his mother and also the Duke have not nurtured him
And so Caliban is the innocent one.

Emma Weir (14)
Methodist College

What's Happening To Me?

What's happening to me?
I'm stuck in this rainforest
At the dead of night
Wanting to get some sleep
But can't, in fear of the cold
Is that a snake near me?

What's happening to me?
I'm stuck in this tropical sea
Desperately trying to swim
Stopped by the lifejacket
Gradually pushing me down
Down in the greenish blue.

What's happening to me?
I'm seat belted into an air plane seat
Accelerating downwards
All around me, panic reigns
What the tannoy screams 'Brace, brace'
I dip my head waiting for impact.

What's happening to me?
I'm stuck in my own mind again.

Robert Todd (15)
Methodist College

The Art Of Writing Poetry

So you think it's hard to write a poem?
One that looks and sounds just right?
I can't do it! It never works!
Yes you can, you just have to try.

It can be silly . . .
I woke up to the cock crow one morning
And the wafting aroma of bacon and eggs,
In slippers I padded down to the kitchen
And my father was waxing his legs.

My old mother was planning a stag night
And my brother was plaiting his hair
The baby was cooking my breakfast
The entire scene gave me a scare!

Or serious . . .
It's still there, in the back of your mind,
It never lets up, the dull, concentrated pain.
You wake up and everything's alright
. . . Until you remember.

It hits you like a lightning bolt
And you can feel the bile rise
The nausea washes over you
Like a raging sea on the stony strand.

Not one second goes by when she doesn't occupy your mind.
Her fiery red hair, and her piercing green eyes, like sparkling pools.
Her caring hands and consoling words, with the lilting French accent.
And her voice . . . oh her voice . . .

Your whole body is numb
And you hate yourself more
. . . For killing her

It's the Art of Writing Poetry.

Sarah Martin (14)
Methodist College

SURFING

I see the rough sea water,
a board tucked under my arm.
The waves crash all around
as, the clouds get darker and darker
with rolls of thunder and flashes of light.

I dip my feet in and feel the cold
I wade on in engulfed in seaweed
In the distance I can see the illuminous colours
Bobbing up and down
Suddenly they disappear.

I see them racing towards me
Swaying from side to side
On the right two fall down
But the others keep on coming
Smashing over the water.

Water sprays up behind them
And through they go
But the last one falls down
And drifts to shore
Now it's my turn.

Mark Ferguson (14)
Methodist College

CALIBAN

There was a man called Caliban.
A cruel and grotesque man he was.
Brought up as a child he had no morals,
Never knew the meaning of right or wrong.
But in a way it was not his fault,
For he has had no one to nurture or care for him,
He had no education or friends
And now because of this he has committed terrible crimes
Where innocent people have had to pay for his lack of thought
And care for other people's feelings.

And now as a slave, he is alone.
With only the sweet sounds of music to comfort him.
Me, I do not hate or dislike Caliban,
But feel sorry for and pity him,
That he has grown into such an ugly beast.
Wandering around unintelligent and confused,
Lustful and selfish, he shows no remorse for his crimes.
And now he is trapped alone on an island
To spend his days isolated from the world,
Never to know what it is really like to live
And never to find out the meaning of life.

Lauren Donaghy (14)
Methodist College

CALIBAN THE BEAST

Caliban sat thinking of what he could have had,
He could have been king of the Island,
He could have been Prospher's master,
Miranda could have been his wife.

If only he killed Prospero,
He would be ruler,
If only he destroyed his magic,
He would be king.

Oh my Miranda,
How beautiful she looks,
If only he murdered Prospero,
She would be his.

And what of his mother Sycorax,
What was she like,
She was the only one who loved him,
And she left him what she loved.

Now he has no one to love,
No one to love him,
He is just an ugly slave,
Who would . . . want him?

Scott Thompson (13)
Methodist College

CALIBAN'S POEM

The island was lonely and deserted,
until Prospero and Miranda come,
they come by craft with no provisions or sails, but driven by the wind.
On the Isle lives Caliban - an ugly beast and the magical Ariel,
Prospero has brought magic upon this island.

There is darkness before Prospero and Miranda arrive,
there is darkness in the witch Sycorax, who cared not for
her son or for the island but only for herself.
The island of strange mysteries, its haunted woods and its howling
cries, now has been filled with the sound of a sweet soft melody.

The island is almost filled with light, the darkness has almost faded and
the clouds are the colour gold.
The sun shines and the sea glistens.
In shame and anger Caliban hides himself away from Prospero.
Caliban serves Prospero for doing wrong to Miranda.

Caliban is like a wild beast, he is angry and scared of Prospero.
His horrendous stench and repulsive features make him a monster.
He is helpless and alone,
yet he appreciates the sweet music of the isle.

Susannah Gleadhill (13)
Methodist College

MY MUM

She changed my nappies, she fed me
She put me to bed and clothed me
She was my Santa, she was my tooth fairy
My mum was the one who made me.

Forcing myself to remember these things
Gritting my teeth to stop myself speaking
She goes on and on about life and future
'Who cares?' I think. 'It's my life.'

She drones on about teenagers
Schools aren't strict enough, she says
You go out too much, you're far too young
I wonder, 'When will she ever quit?'

But deep down in my heart
A little voice tells me,
'You love her really'
For I know I'll never find another like her.

Hyun-Kyoung Koo (15)
Methodist College

CALIBAN

He came from a magical land,
A mysteriously enchanting, gold kissed island.
A shimmering isle, filled with music and harmony,
A beautiful place, but a prison to him.

Trapped by the sorcerer, tricked and defeated,
An animal like creature, hiding in his dwelling.
Grotesque and angry, he is now a slave.
Alone and lonely, uncivilised and beastly,
He seems vile and ugly, a repulsive creature.

But he had no mother to teach him discipline and morals.
He grew up not knowing right from wrong,
He does not understand good and bad.
He was left alone to learn to survive.
He had no teacher, no one to look up to,
So how could his badness be all his fault?

Louise Waugh (13)
Methodist College

The Creature Of The Isle

Over a crystal sparkling sea,
A land of wonder lies awaiting thee.
A land of colour; music and grace,
Never before trod upon by any race.
But there is an exception to most rules,
Here it is Caliban over whom loneliness looms.
A beastly creature he may seem,
But appreciates all land, sound and stream.
Though upon the isle one day landed Prospero from far away.
A friend for the animal he did make,
Though a risky step did Caliban take.
Filled with lust and inner fire,
To violate Miranda was his heart's desire.
Prospero with anger he did fill,
Caliban the monster he would kill!
Now however a better thought finds the sorcerer's head,
Why should he not enslave the beast instead?
Prospero now master of the uncivilised beast,
Friendly thoughts of each other now did cease.
Caliban as you would find is a simple soul,
His position unimportant and an unrespected role.
Son of a witch since deceased,
Untaught of manners was this beast.
Full of hate, he was indeed,
When Prospero was gone he would be free.
Now on the island left to roam,
Is Caliban all alone.
Now his visitors leave without a smile,
And we say goodbye,
To the creature of the isle.

Neil Dunn (14)
Methodist College

CALIBAN

On a small unknown island,
Somewhere between Naples and Milan,
There lives a monster like creature,
Named Caliban.

This magical island is full of haunting music,
And mysterious sounds.
On this isle lives a powerful enchanter called Prospero,
He lives on the mystical isle with his daughter Miranda,
And the monster like creature named Caliban.

Caliban is Prospero's vile slave,
Caliban's mother Sycorax once ruled the isle,
But now Prospero the powerful enchanter,
Rules the mysterious isle.

Caliban can be spiteful and mean,
But this is because he is a very lonely creature.
I think Caliban is musical and loving,
But on the outside he is disgustingly ugly.

Caliban is like this because of his mother Sycorax.
She taught him to be selfish and sinister.
Caliban would not be like this,
If he was brought up differently.

Inside Caliban is very confused,
And he is also gullible and vulnerable.
Caliban is very different on the inside,
Compared to his outside appearance.

Carole Wilson (14)
Methodist College

ONE SPECIAL EVE

Not a sound.
The small child lies awake in the soothing silence.
His stimulated eyes dart and dash across the room.
Soon a whisper whistles lightly from the rooftops -
A pattern of apprehension and excitement crosses the child's face.
He raises his dutiful head, to see if he has yet struck upon his goldmine.

The clipping of visitors' shoes is what he can imagine to be above.
He has been waiting for this night to come for days,
Weeks and even months.
He had prepared a treat for them, ready on the table.
Four pairs of saucers stand present and correct for the arriving party.
The child lay his head on his pillow in wonder -
Whatever would he say to his welcome guests?

His guest of honour is the most special of the well-known group.
He would enter the boy's house by the black, dirty tunnel
And come wearing a bold velvet robe that never fades.
His long white curls shall reach down from his chin.
He would come the bearer of sweet surprises
And a special plate lies in store, but for only him.

The child's head soothes deeper into his soft headrest,
As he imagines how he'd greet his friends on their
Entrance to his home.
But only the warmth of his body seeps through to his head.
Soon a translucent figure leads the newcomer through the tall gate
And into the walled sheets of slumber.

Matthew Bell (14)
Methodist College

SENSATIONS

The rising of the sun, the fall of the night
Can inspire a waking mind,
A world bursting with many things
Which add to human kind.

A child's laugh, a rustle in the trees
Will brighten up your day
And give to you the happy sounds
Which fulfil our lives this way.

The waft of fresh bread, tea brewing in the pot,
Can create a pleasant mood.
These relaxing aromas are encircling us
In the high streets, homes and woods.

The coarseness of wood, the smoothness of silk,
For at a loss we all would be
If everything was flat and square
There would be no variety.

The creaminess of milk, the sweetness of fruit
Provide us with many flavours
From harvest, Christmas and summer cuisine,
All are there for us to savour.

Feeling a presence, a shiver up your spine
Can provoke a spooky notion,
For there are many things misunderstood
Which can play with our emotions.

Sensations are wonderful things
Which fill the mind, body and soul.
However, we must enjoy them while they last
As they are quick to come and go.

Laura Collins (14)
Methodist College

BELLS AND UNWELLS

A letter in the post
Brought me the news,
I was to be a flower-girl
And skip past all the pews.

Along came the day,
When I got into that dress,
Climbed into the car,
Trying not to look a mess.

A black-suited man
Lifted me over a puddle,
While everybody else
Got into a muddle.

Up the aisle
Without fail,
But illness struck
And I began to wail.

Rushing out of the church
And down the street,
With my mum asking,
'What did you eat?'

After a few moments,
It was all clear,
With everybody saying,
'Oh, the poor dear!'

Deborah Boyd (14)
Methodist College

WHEN I WENT TO WAR

I left my house in early morn,
the goodbyes were said and off I went.

I became cold, scared and hungry,
the travelling made me tired.

The day of tense preparation ended,
a large rock became my uncomfortable bed.

We had to wake up in the early hours,
this would be our day of destiny.

Rifles were given out like they were toys,
but this was certainly no game.

All troops were in brand new uniform,
it was one massive field of green.

Then we saw the enemy,
as fast as lightning we were in formation.

With a violent bang it started,
I was shaking like a leaf.

There was death, pain and bloodshed,
the bravery was hard to believe.

It was clear we had the upper hand,
but it was at dear cost.

After a couple of hours of determination,
news filtered through that we had won.

That night there was no joy or celebrations,
our thoughts were with those who couldn't celebrate.

Andrew McIntyre (13)
Methodist College

The Night!

As a beholder of the darkness, I see images of lights forming an
illustration in the distance.
I see shadows and opaque objects
Creatures arise and people creep quietly as the sun moves out of
visibility and minds sink to rest.
Thoughts pause as the eye closes,
the dreams escape and the nightmares yell and dominate
as the atmosphere crystallises and the mood stills.
The light is drawn gently from human eyes once again.
The night air falls on my once heated skin making me feel cold
and my breath visual.
The silence is forsake.
The silence is frightening.
The cold breeze moves gradually and will have reached its objective
before the warm, orange sun returns.
The phantoms of the imagination are discharged as the streets die
and the twilight dwells.
And as the human race falls, I gaze out of my window thinking clearly
and craving for the sun, the heat and the light to return.
My eyes close slowly
as I become a victim of . . . The Night!

Matthew Crosby (15)
Methodist College

Love, Hate

I love my family more than anything,
They cherish, protect, understand and listen.
Yet, I don't like them all the time.
They whinge, moan, whimper and groan.

I don't spend enough time with my family,
They are fun, adventurous, exciting and happy,
Yet, I can't get rid of them fast enough.
They forbid, admonish, prevent and punish.

I feel like an important part of my family,
They include, accept, respect and support.
Yet, I am different from them.
They frustrate, irritate, aggravate and alienate.

I love my family, I don't always want them,
I don't spend enough time with my family, I see them too much.
I am an important member of my family, I feel like I don't count.
I am part of them, they are part of me.

Eleanor Gilmore (15)
Methodist College

SOME PEOPLE!

I long to stare deep inside your eyes,
To delve beneath your actor's mask,
To unleash the truths which must lie beyond,
A concoction of fears, loves, hates and dreams.

Amongst the grey cloud which is your macho exterior,
A silver lining is visible to me.
I can see the warm heat beneath your cold words,
The dreams behind your blank face.

To lower the drawbridge and let me into your world,
Would in your eyes be to admit defeat.

Why must everything in your life be a game?

Victoria Mackay (15)
Methodist College

Mum

We sometimes had an argument,
A fight, a silly feud.
She never admitted that she was wrong
And I really wished she would.

We fought about clothes, about money,
About what time I stayed out to.
She disliked my circle of friends.
She never saw my point of view.

But as I grew older and wiser,
Day by day,
I realised that she'd be there for me
In every different way.

She comforted me and laughed with me,
She held me near
When I needed it and
Wiped away a stray tear.

Gone was the annoying, nagging mum,
And in her place was a kind-hearted woman
That I had never noticed before.

Laura Grant (14)
Methodist College

IGNORANCE

What am I?

I breed hatred, anger and racism,
I bring war to humanity,
I burn whole cities to the ground,
I destroy ethnic minorities, and drive them from their homes,
I create horrible sights of hundreds of bloody bodies,
I bring terrible new weapons which cause mass destruction.

But worst of all, I bring death.
Pointless, useless deaths of innocent people.
I cause mourning families and friends, and broken lives.
I cause pollution and the destruction of the earth,
And I destroy whole species of animals,
And burn forests to the ground.

I am a part of everyone,
Slowly starting to die over thousands of years,
But I am not yet dead, or dying quickly enough.
What am I?
Am I the devil?
No, I am ignorance.

Steven Christie (13)
Methodist College

GIRL

They see this girl the five school days,
Some see her as confident, outgoing and fun.
But can they imagine a side hidden from view,
Vulnerable and tender, only ever seen by a few.

Could they think of her when sitting alone
Remembering her heartache and ever-lingering pain.
Despite her young age, she can't forget all her fears,
The tragedy and sorrow, she has seen through the years.

When she's among them, these people she knows,
Smiling and nodding pretending everything's fine.
Feeling inadequate, disliked and insecure,
Someone please hold her, in a way only for her.

Anger and bitterness are all on her mind,
People she loves, gone from her life.
She's happy, yet sad; whole but incomplete,
These emotions come to everyone, until their days meet.

Softly she remembers those wonderful days
Buried inside her, beneath all the gloom,
Brought to the surface by those very people
With her all day, past, present and future.

Judith Pollock (14)
Methodist College

TENNIS

Imagine this; it's July,
It's very, very hot,
The crowds are arriving happy and expectant,
The players are nervous, happy and afraid,
But all are enjoying a great day out,
You don't have to imagine,
Go to Wimbledon!

Centre court is packed,
Strawberries and cream are bought and eaten,
Players are warming up.
Thump, twang, bounce. Thump, twang, bounce.
'Please take your seats,'
The match has begun.

Bound, bounce, bounce . . . Thump, twang, bounce,
'Fault'
Bounce, bounce, bounce . . .Thump, twang, bounce,
Thump, twang bounce. Thump, twang, 'Out.'
Gasps and cheers erupt. Bounce, bounce, bounce.
The repetitions go on and on, uninterrupted.
Finally, it's match point.
Silence.

Bounce, bounce, bounce, thump, twang, bounce,
Thump, twang, bounce, thump, twang, thump, twang, bounce.
It's a long rally, back and forth, on and on.
Suddenly . . . 'Out!' Cheers erupt, whistling, cheering and clapping,
Emotions are flying,
The winner; happy, smiling thoughts of money, fame and
achievement of dreams,
The loser: 'Out?', thoughts of money, fame and achievement of dreams.
It's all over again . . .
Until next year that is.

Christopher Sanlon (14)
. Methodist College

THIRTY YEARS OF HURT

The streets are full of murder and blood,
Instead of children and play.
The government sends fleets of police
To try to keep the fragile peace.

Drumcree has come for another year,
Police are prepared for the worst,
At night, the rioters start the trouble
In a hateful Portadown.

Bullets, bombs and baseball bats
From Shankhill to Ardoyne,
Whether it be for God and Ulster
Or for some simple cause.

Tears are falling like the rain
And funerals cram down streets,
Mothers weeping at lonely graves
And grief is bitter-sweet.

Kris McConkey (14)
Orangefield High School

THE TROUBLES

The streets used to be full of joy
and children playing wildly,
but over the past twenty-five years
it has been full of murderous scenes.

The bands are marching freely
for this time of year,
as the sectarian violence
grows ever near.

The Ormeau Road protesters
are sitting on their road,
while the Orangemen are protesting
because they can't get down the Garvachy Road.

Brendan McKenna is smiling
and is probably wearing a crown,
but I assure you that we will
get marching down Portadown.

Raymond Jordan (14)
Orangefield High School

HALLOWE'EN

Hallowe'en is very near,
lots and lots to fear.
Ghosts and vampires, goblins too,
which one of these will get you?

Witches on their brooms,
little kids hiding in their rooms
as the unholy looms.

Fireworks being lit,
blown up every bit,
bright colours in the sky
as witches fly by.

Are you really scared?
Monsters might get you,
so be prepared.

David Hogg (14)
Orangefield High School

WINTER

Jack Frost comes once again,
Hats, gloves and scarves are getting put on,
Snow and ice cause accidents,
Santa Claus comes on Christmas Eve,
Children hang up their stockings.
Children leave milk and biscuits for Santa
And a carrot for Rudolph.
New Year's Eve parties are booming,
New Year's day, everyone is dying from the night before,
Everyone makes New Year's promises.
4th January, children start back at school
After their Christmas holidays.

Susan Forsythe (12)
Orangefield High School

THE 007 DREAM

I've had a dream
Since I was eleven
That one day
I might be 007.
I'd battle the evil Doctor No,
Over in the snow,
I'd rescue the damsels in distress
And take them over to the
wild, wild west.

Colin Wellington (11)
Orangefield High School

WINTER

It is snowy,
It is rainy
And it gets boring.
People build snowmen
And have snow fights
In the windy old nights.

Jonathan Connolly (11)
Orangefield High School

MY WISH

I wish that all the cease-fires would always stay intact.
I wish that we could live in peace and not in fear for our lives.
I wish that all the shooting would just stop.
I wish that Protestants and Catholics could live in peace and harmony.
I wish there could be agreement, that both sides would adore.
I wish that some day all the parades' re-routing would stop.
And I wish that all my wishes would come true.

Glen Blackmore (13)
Orangefield High School

SUMMER

In the sun it is lovely and hot,
It feels like a boiling pot.
I would like to be in the shade
Or on the beach with my bucket and spade.
In the open with a cold drink,
Beside a swimming pool, I think.

Steven Burns (11)
Orangefield High School

CHRISTMAS

Remember, remember, the 25th of December
When Santa came to my house.
He brought me a soccer set and a knockout kit
And brought my sister a mouse.
He brought my mummy new clothes
And my daddy got Rudolph's nose.
He ate his cookies and drank his milk
And put on h is coat, which was silk.
Now remember, all you need to do
Is write a note and make it float
All the way to the North Pole.

Chris Murphy (11)
Orangefield High School

BELFAST MORNINGS

A cold winter's morning,
Children in hats, scarves and big coats,
Ice on the footpaths and the roads,
Street lights were shining in the morning sky,
I snuggle up in bed with my hot water bottle,
Gritter lorries throwing grit on the roads,
Steam rises as the children sweat in their scarves,
Suddenly, the clouds separate and the sun jumps up
And melts away the ice.
Belfast is bright again.

Nikki Robinson (12)
Orangefield High School

WINTER

Christmas time is here,
Presents are given,
Young children throw snowballs,
It's Jesus' birthday.

The children open their presents,
Their eyes full of joy, everything they want is there,
It's Christmas.

Animals all gather up food,
They hide in holes, trees
And many other things.
They cuddle together
Snug as a bug in a rug.

Then snow falls, children have fights
And make snowmen so bright,
Ten men's cars froze,
Cars lights flash because it's night.

The long nights arrive,
It's cold out there,
but when bed time comes,
You forget everything.

The tree goes up, people decorate it,
They put on lights, bells and a fairy at the top,
January comes,
Decorations come down,
Christmas is over for another year.

Pamela Todd (12)
Orangefield High School

A Ghost Ship Never Forgotten

It was a cold night and it was the 14th April,
The death of a titan.
For many years, sailors said the seas were haunted
By the dead, but I thought it was an old myth.
It was late, close to midnight, then I heard a fog horn
That was so loud the windows broke.
From nowhere, mist was sprouting from the dark waters
Sending a chill down my spine.
All of a sudden, a ship appeared from the mist and
The side of this great ship was badly damaged,
But it floated perfectly.
After I saw the great vessel and iceberg came from the mist
And what happened next? The great ship collided with the iceberg.
The ship and the iceberg passed each other,
But the ship was sinking into the water.
From nowhere, screams and fireworks came from the mist
That scared my soul.
An hour later, the great ship sank.
Just one glance from my eye, I saw an old lifesaver,
Saying SS Titanic.

Mark Warren (13)
Orangefield High School

War

On the war line the enemy are driving us back,
But we still stand strong.
The fear of death is in us all.

The hundreds of our men running to the front line,
Paratroopers getting shot as they glide through the air.

Machine gun bullets dropping to the ground,
people dying in awful ways.

Our tanks coming in and driving them back.
I heard shouting, 'We've won.'
I stood up and cheered.

Andrew Patterson (12)
Orangefield High School

THE EMPTY HOUSE

The house is quiet now there's no one here
It's cold and dark I tremble with fear
What was that sound, a creaking door
Footsteps maybe on the wooden floor.

Is it ghouls or spectres abroad at night
I turn to see, I get a fright.
I can't describe what it is I've seen
My mouth fell open I tried to scream.

But my voice did make no sound
My body it was never found
Now I walk these empty halls,
Passing quietly through the walls
Doomed to spend eternity all because of my curiosity.

I saw the house with its open door
An invitation to explore
But now I mourn that fateful day
And wished to God I'd stayed away.

Pamela Connolly (14)
Orangefield High School

Hallowe'en

Hallowe'en comes on the 31st October.
It comes once a year,
I'll be glad when it's over.
Fireworks and rockets that go off late at night,
when you're in bed it's such a big fright.

The children go trick or treating at night,
door to door their lanterns so bright.
We give them some goodies for their delight.
They run round corners out of sight.

The moon is shining
high in the sky.
The witches are flying
with their cats close by.
Higher and higher and higher
they fly, up and away
into the dark, dark, sky.

Trudie Curran (13)
Orangefield High School

My Love

My love is so, so gorgeous,
I care for him very much,
His face you could touch,
He just speaks like us.

His hair shines like sunlight,
And eyes are sparkly blue,
He always wears trendy clothes,
And smells like a red rose.

He's no fat or thin,
He is just in between
And he's never, never mean,
He is just nice and clean.

Carrie Martin (12)
Orangefield High School

SUMMER FUN

Summer is a time of fun
No homework's to be done
All the children go out to play
On the nice summer's day.

Long summer evenings
Short summer nights
Children play in the sun
They are all very bright.

Lots of families go away
To enjoy the summer days
Adults lie about in the sun
While their children have some fun.

People go to beaches
To lie in the sun
But when they come home
They are burnt like a bun.

But when night falls
The children cry out
That's what summer
Is all about.

Laura McBride (14)
Orangefield High School

HAUNTED HOUSE

I came out one day,
My terrible sister ran away,
I came up to this house
That was as quiet as a mouse.
I opened the creaky gate,
I walked up to my fate!

I knocked on the door,
There came a very loud roar.
The door was open a little inch,
I peeped in, over my head flew a finch.
It made me jump in a very big way,
It lead me into the hallway.

I saw a dining table and some food,
I couldn't resist it, it looked so good.
I got closer but I couldn't stop,
There were cakes, sandwiches, juice
And an ice-cream lollipop.
I ignored the food and walked on.
I came up to this bright light,
Wow, it really shone.

It brought me to the front door.
I opened it and walked out,
Without a doubt,
I'll never return there again!

Louise Bell (12)
Orangefield High School

My Christmas Poem

Look at the Christmas tree standing tall.
All wrapped in decorations you'd think it was about to fall.
Oh how lovely is the snow lying all around
I can see it falling from the sky to the ground.
There is that lovely smell again.
It makes me feel safe as I am far away
from that snowy rain.

It's morning time again.
The snowy rain has seemed to stop
But as I walk downstairs
I stand in amazement at the presents lying there.
Once the presents are open and done.
Now Christmas is over we'll have to wait another year.

Ashley McFarland (12)
Orangefield High School

Summer

Summer is the time when bird sing,
Flaming hot days,
Smell of freshly cut grass,
Bonfires blazing,
Smells of barbecues,
Clear, blue skies,
Days are long, nights are short,
Having parties all night long.

Louis Tittensor (12)
Orangefield High School

WINTER AND CHRISTMAS

Christmas is a time of joy
When Mary had her baby boy
We all have lots of fun
When the winter has begun.

We all play in the snow
While the Christmas tree lights glow
Santa is on his way
He is coming on his sleigh.

We have lots of parties
And children are eating Smarties
We get new clothes
And wine overflows.

Gemma Bowers (12)
Orangefield High School

MY POEM ABOUT MY FAMILY

My Uncle Joe's out fishing,
My granny is at the mall,
While my granda is at the club,
My dad is at the pub,
While my mum is out with Mark,
I am lying in my bedroom,
All alone in the dark.

Robert Speers (12)
Orangefield High School

MACBETH

Swords wave in the air
Blood trickles down a field
A day so foul and fair
There two men stand behind shields
They are Macbeth and Banquo.

Banquo beat on his drum
Macbeth's sword rips through a vein
Spurting blood and pain
After the battle is won Banquo beats on his drum

They meet three witches
One she has thirty-two toes
One she has a wart on her nose
One is crooked and fell
Three horrid demons from Hell.

A dagger appears before his eyes
He listens to the devil's lies
And good King Duncan cruelly dies.

Macbeth becomes king
With his evil queen
He rules with fear and terror
There's blood on the thistle and heather.

Macbeth dies, no one sighs
MacDuff puts his head on a sword
The tyrant has gone the action is done
And Malcom is King and Lord.

Down in Hell where the flames leap high
And the blood runs down the walls
The red-hot heat and the smell of deceit
Pandemonium falls.

Craig Greer (15)
Orangefield High School

I'M SICK OF

I'm sick of living to defend myself,
I'm sick of having really bad health,
I'm sick of lacking good wealth,
I'm sick of spoofers and the people that believe what they say,
I'm sick of being hired and fired the very same day
I'm sick of looking at my mum for pay,
I'm sick of people saying there's only one way,
I'm sick of the wrong people being jolly and gay,
I'm sick of everybody being really, really mean,
And of best friends not being what they seem,
I'm sick of being sucked in by Satan's tractor beam,
I'm sick of kissing the face of death and being pushed
                                in further by life itself.

Marco Chambers (14)
Orangefield High School

HALLOWE'EN

Hallowe'en a spooky time
When all your doorbells start to chime
With little children all dressed up
Carrying a little charity cup.
People screaming most of them scared
And everyone has been dared
To go to little Tommy's house
To scare his mum with a mouse.

Amy King (12)
Orangefield High School

TAG TEAM WRESTLING

The lights go out and the music will start.
The crowd is confused in the dark.
Some fireworks go off and the crowd cheers
Then suddenly a man appears.

He is seven feet tall and very scary.
His opponent is feeling weary.
He steps over the top rope into the ring
The crowd starts to chant and sing.

The bell has rung and the gag is made
That huge man standing in the shade.
If you wish to know this wrestler's name
You will call him of the name of Kane.

His five-foot partner X-pac starts the fight.
With not a punch to see in sight.
There were headlocks, take-downs and suplexes too
There were some pins but very few.

Near the end of the math he was near defeat.
He knew if he didn't tag Kane was beat.
X-pac made the tag and in came Kane
Taking down everyone again and again.

Kane cured his fury by giving a choke slam
Then X-pac got a tag for more mayhem.
He knocked them out hoping for glory
Then he pinned them 1, 2, 3, that's the end of my story.

David Blair (12)
Orangefield High School

THE HAUNTED HOUSE

Not far away from my street
there's a house that smells like people's feet.
The house that would scare you away
that would make you go mentally insane.

I went to it one day
and something scared me away
but I went back yesterday
I was as quiet as a mouse
when I saw a living thing in the house.
I ran and ran as fast as I could
I looked back and saw a little man wearing a hood.

He was see-through not that scary though,
I thought I was dead
because I accidentally bumped my head.
I talked to him for a little while
then I went home and cried and cried
because of his little story
I hope he finds some glory.

Alana Bell (12)
Orangefield High School

WITCHES

Hallowe'en night
the stars are bright
and witches haunt the sky

With their black cats
and broomsticks
they fly and fly and fly.

They fly back to the castles
and fill their cauldrons high
with carts and dogs
and fish and frogs

The poison
makes them fly.

Stacey Youll (14)
Orangefield High School

THE TROUBLES

Boom goes the bomb
Everybody is in shock
Glass is flying everywhere
Blood is draining out of people
Innocent people are being killed.

Police surrounded the streets
Land Rovers on every street corner
Men with balaclavas up street corners
Run so they won't be caught
Forgetting about the good things they were taught
As they do a bolt.

If these people do get caught
By the wrong people they will be shot.
By the right people they will be jailed
But I don't think any of them want to be nailed.

David McConkey (14)
Orangefield High School

HALLOWE'EN

Hallowe'en is coming
The children come out to play
Parties on all night long
And fireworks on display.
Dunking for apples is fun
And dressing up is too.
Children are really happy
They have no school to go to,
The Devil comes out to play
And witches, vampires too.
The pumpkin sits there laughing
You must feel really scared and
Don't know what to do.
Hallowe'en is in autumn
Where the leaves fall on the ground.
The children rustle through the leaves
And play amongst the taller trees.

Sarah Moore (12)
Orangefield High School

ANGELS

I saw a flock of angels,
in the heavens up above.
They saw that I was lonely
and had no one to love.

So they took a piece of grass so green
and a piece of sky so blue.
They blended them together
and ended up with you.

Now I'm not so lonely
and have someone to love.
Thanks to all the angles
in the heavens up above.

Annette Girvin (14)
Orangefield High School

SUMMER HOLIDAYS

Children getting off from school
going out and having fun.
Having parties all night long
with a good party song.

Dance clubs open all night long
watch the dope being passed along.
Drink and drugs are doing harm
most victims get sent to the 'funny farm'.

Going on family holiday
oh what fun that must be.
Lying by the beach
watching people play.

People having sleepovers
to stay up all night long.
To make ourselves sick
by drinking all night long.

Holiday days are over
school has come again.
Now I'm back to school
I'll never drink again.

Michelle McCausland (15)
Orangefield High School

Hallowe'en

On Hallowe'en the night is dark,
Then the fireworks start to spark,
There is a big full moon that night,
The children start to run to our doors.
I always get a big fright
I see parties everywhere,
We give them lots of sweets and
Send them on their way.
Hallowe'en is a very bright night
And I always get a big fright.

Sammy-Joe Smith (11)
Orangefield High School

Drugs

Some people smoke dope
Some people take E's
Some people take Magics
But in the end
It all comes to an end
Rapping at death's door.
I need to take more
But what the hell for.
I should try not to take more
Because I don't want to see more gore.

Mark Carson (14)
Orangefield High School

STRIFE

The trouble has been
here for years.
Innocent people
still have fears.

What they say
they will simply do.
Brave Ulsterman
loyal and true!

Some men watching
behind bar cells
simply waiting until
the Peace Process dwells.

Disbanded not!
The RUC.
Peace in Ireland
we hope to see.

Blowing up buildings
just for fun,
but, yet do they know
they're still on the run.

But, now my poem
must come to an end.
Just pray and hope
for peace my friend.

Christine Andrews (15)
Orangefield High School

ULSTER IN JULY

Streets stand quiet
As people wait to riot.
Police stand waiting
As people go beating.

Grown ups die, kids cry
While bands march by.
Flags flutter high
In the clear blue sky.

A final whistle goes
Another building blows
As more destruction grows
But nobody knows
When peace in Ireland will show.

Selene McKeown (14)
Orangefield High School

HALLOWE'EN

The cold nights of school
Come with frights,
The sweets and treats
And the terrible trouble.

The goblins and ghosts
Make horrible toasts
And all the little pussies
Are very juicy.

Glenn Tann (11)
Orangefield High School

My Good Friend

Everybody's so mixed up about love these days,
And everybody's trying to work out in different ways.
What I need from you friend is a good conversation
To put my mind at ease.
An old friend called the other day
And I wasn't quite sure what to say.
She didn't seem to know me anymore
And I said don't treat me as if I'm something new,
I'm still the same old person you used to talk to.
But all I need from you friend, is a long talk again
And we will be back to the same old people again
Not some lonely strangers
That we were some days ago.

Leanne Macey-Lillie (15)
Orangefield High School

The Tigress

The tigress sways from side to side,
Vigilantly watching her new born cubs
With all eagle's eye,
She sees them for off frolicking carefree
Under the shade of an ancient twisted tree,
Suddenly the thunder of hooves echoes in
Her ear drums, the earth is rumbling beneath her.
She runs with all her might to get
The tiger, her partner.
They run across the dusty surface of the plains,
They grabbed the cubs by the scuff.
The cubs cuddle against their parents
Looking for protection.

Lisa Conlane (12)
Orangefield High School

HALLOWE'EN

Vampire, witches, bats and masks
They've all got to do these tasks
Apples on a stick covered in toffee
Gets stuck in your throat and makes you cough.
Dress up and they go try
To scare the children, make them cry.
See the witches on their brooms,
Fly really fast, fly over the moon.
Look at the bats, they fly so high
They'll go up and touch the sky.
The night is over, time for bed
You say to yourself
'Goodnight sleepy head.'
That night I dreamt of next Hallowe'en
I really wished that's where I had been.

Heather Gorman (11)
Orangefield High School

CHRISTMAS

Christmas comes once a year,
Santa and his reindeers will appear
Decorations on our Christmas tree
Brings a lot of cheer to me.
Toys and presents we like to get
Snow is here, don't forget.
The turkey is here for us to eat
I really think Christmas is a treat.

Kirsty Davidson (11)
Orangefield High School

OUT OF SCHOOL

Three o'clock strikes
The bell rings
Then the doors fly open
The children rush out.

With a wild cat call,
A surging crowd like a whirling top
And a hop, hop, hop.

Grazing of knees
A hair pull and a slap
A hitched-up satchel
Then I saw the bulldog.
He ran for me
But I ran all the way home.

Graham Wallace
Orangefield High School

AUTUMN

A ll the leaves fall off the trees
U nder the ground sleep all the animals
T wigs have broke off the trees
U p in the sky there is a full moon
M onsters are out for Hallowe'en
N ightime falls every early.

Mark McConnell
Orangefield High School

HALLOWE'EN

The fireworks go bang
The parties start
People trick or treat
And the schools are off.

The sun goes down
The moon comes up
Witches flying about the sky
Monsters on the ground
Ghosts flying and walking
About every single town.

Werewolves are howling
Then the fireworks go off
And scare all scary things away.

The ghosts disappear
The witches fly home
Monsters go back to their dens
The zombies go back to their graves
And werewolves go back to their caves.

Craig Magee (11)
Orangefield High School

HALLOWE'EN

Hallowe'en is the best,
Fireworks, ghosts and ghouls
And even scary masks
Going to a party to some silly tasks!

Black cats, vamps and spiders too
All come hunting just for you,
Sounds in the night
It's a scary sight!

Hiding underneath the covers of your bed
Creepy noises you hear instead,
To scared to take a look
But in the end it's just a book!

But don't, don't take any chances,
Creepy feelings in your mind
So whatever you do, don't look behind.

Darren Birch (12)
Orangefield High School

I Look Out My Window

I look out my window and what do I see?
A big bare tree looking at me.
Its leaves all brown and crusty
Falling off when it's musty.

I look out my window and what do I see?
A big bare tree looking at me
But wait!
The leaves are all back, it blooms so bright.
Until one horrible summer's night,
A noise of chopping wood near by
When I looked I tried not to cry
The trees I've seen for many years
Now no birds' songs can fill my ears.

Gina Kennedy (13)
Orangefield High School

THE DINGO

Its eyes glinted faintly as it moved its head from side to side
Gazing stealthily over the plain
It paused and hung its nose in the air to catch an
Intriguing scent.
Suddenly, the animal froze
Its tongue lolled and saliva dripped from its hungry mouth
It spots a lamb far off.
It slowly moves towards its prey
It bends down ready to pounce
Suddenly it bolts
A hunting party
The lamb lives to see tomorrow.

Danielle Dickey (11)
Orangefield High School

AUTUMN

The rain comes in and leaves change colour.
To red, orange, gold, brown and yellow too.
School starts and kids go to school for another year.
Church services start to thank God for
Everything in the world.
Then Hallowe'en comes and kids dress up like
Witches and devils, ghosts and other beasts
And go out trick or treating and play games
Like dunking for apples and hitting the horse for sweets.
Then farmers go out to harvest the crops
For people all over the world and for us as well.

Ashley McKay (12)
Orangefield High School

MY SOUL'S EYE

My eye is bleeding
The window to my soul is broken
You can now see my innermost thoughts
I have no secrets, nothing to hide
Everything I have done and am going to do
Is visible, open to scrutiny
Please don't criticise me
My thoughts are fragile
My mind is a strained glass window
Painted with details of my life
Leaded with my experiences
Criticism is a stone
It will shatter my mind
And all the work that I,
The artist have put into it
My life is before you
Look but please don't touch
Your interference may have
Adverse effects.
Just because you can see it
Doesn't mean it's yours to play with
All my emotions are here
Love, hate, joy, sorrow
There is no mystery to me now
My cover has been blown
I have lost all faith in my mind
My rage is building
But you can see it coming
And you avoid its volatile manifestation
Because . . . my eye is bleeding.

Chris McWilliams (15)
Our Lady And St Patrick's College

HALLOWE'EN'S COMING!

The night becomes dark and scary,
Superstitious people become very wary.
Children go to trick or treat,
Just looking for money or something to eat.

A full moon in the sky,
Mothers baking their apple pies.
Wolves howling in the woods,
While the kids are eating their food.

Witches fly in the sky,
Stars sparkling way up high.
Fireworks bang, crackle and pop,
So watch out wherever you go.

Laura McCarthy (14)
Our Lady Of Mercy Secondary School

HALLOWE'EN FOR THE FUTURE VOICES

Witches and goblins both, Hallowe'en bring,
Bangers and bonfires among other things.
Unrecognisable neighbours one does meet,
As dressed-up children play trick or treat.
Doors are rapped and rhymes are recited,
With generous payment the kids are delighted.

Susanne Thomas (13)
Our Lady Of Mercy Secondary School

HALLOWE'EN

Hallowe'en has just begun
All the kids are having fun,
Making a fuss, getting dressed,
To see whose costume is the best.
Wizards, goblins, ghosts and bats
Witches wearing tall black hats.
Lots of costumes are being used
If you're looking for someone, you'll get confused
But the winner was a Millennium Bug
And that's a creature I'd never hug,
So give everyone a big cheer.

Until Hallowe'en comes next year.

Karen Jones (13)
Our Lady Of Mercy Secondary School

THE BANSHEE

She stands beside the gnarled old tree,
A fearful spectre
A scary sight
Howling and screeching late at night.

She puts the fear in all who see
The lady known as the Banshee,
People say when you hear her cry
Someone you know is going to die.

So don't go near the very old tree
Because it's likely you'll meet the banshee.

Grace Smyth (14)
Our Lady Of Mercy Secondary School

It's Hallowe'en Night Year '99

The dark clouds scudded across the sky,
The pale yellow moon provided the light,
A single star glued up so high,
All is still this Hallowe'en night.

A crowd of cheers, some scary sights,
The children paired up in search of treats,
They all went off into the darkness of the night,
With goblins and witches with crooked feet.

It was well after midnight and time for bed.
The parents were enjoying the evening laughter.
The house was warm and the children well fed.
But then a loud noise came from the rafters.

They all went outside to have a look,
To see what the noise was about,
On the rooftops was perched a witch,
She said we had killed her spouse.

So she cast a spell all over the house.

'It will be your last Hallowe'en night

Of this millennium.'

Amanda Shields (13)
Our Lady Of Mercy Secondary School

Doom And Gloom

Hallowe'en night is here
And everyone's in fear
Witches, cats and big black bats
Leave us all in tears.

As the sky gets darker
And the clock strikes 12 o'clock,
The witches were here
And now they have gone
And now we are out of fear.

Deborah Kane (14)
Our Lady Of Mercy Secondary School

HALLOWE'EN NIGHT

The 31st of October, do you know what it means?
Sausages, sweets, bangers and beans.
The fireworks bang and light the sky,
Some are low and some are high.
The children party all night long,
And sing the same old Hallowe'en song.
The food is very nice to eat,
Some are sour and some are sweet.
I dress my brother as a devil,
He looks so ugly and so evil.
I dress my sister as a witch,
She gets some money and thinks she is rich.
Here comes the fireworks, there's a lot,
Here comes the food, it is very hot.
Look at the moon, it is very bright,
I am getting such a fright.
When we play games and someone wins,
Everyone cheers and the winner grins.
We're having a good time,
But dread that chime.
For Hallowe'en to be over.

Aisling Taylor (14)
Our Lady Of Mercy Secondary School

THE WITCH OF HALLOWE'EN

Hallowe'en is now here!
A witch screeches,
It sounds so near,
Across the moon on her broom.
She cackles ha, ha, ha, ha!
Scary features what a sight,
When you see her late at night.

Her jet-black cat sits upon,
Her broom.
Into the distance they quickly zoom.
Looking for children as they go.
Casting spells on the people below.

Emma Gibson (14)
Our Lady Of Mercy Secondary School

BEWITCHED

A cat walked slowly beside the park
Its eyes glowed like emeralds in the dark
Its fur so black, like a night without stars
It prowled round the streets till the early hours.

A witch on a broomstick flew overhead
While some tired children slept in bed
Her cat screeched, while some people preached,
About the dangers of Hallowe'en.

Denise Clarken (13)
Our Lady Of Mercy Secondary School

HALLOWE'EN

Hallowe'en is nearly here,
All the kids are dressing up,
Witches, fairies, princesses and frogs are only
some things that you see.
Monsters, goblins and scary things are just some of the visitors
you meet at your door.
They sing you a song to see what they get money, biscuits,
chocolate and sweets.
Fireworks fly through the sky, the colours fly and they die.
Bangers and Catherine wheels are only some things
that make a noise.
All the dogs are barking and all the kids are crying.
And then all of a sudden the noise goes away the
door stops rapping.

Danielle McAuley (14)
Our Lady Of Mercy Secondary School

WITCHES

Witches all dressed up as scared as can be,
Joined by their wicked black cats.
They prance around their cauldron and cast a spell.
'Hubble, bubble toil and trouble fires burn and cauldrons bubble.'
Then they come out and give you a fright.
Now they fly high . . .
High in the sky and say goodbye.

Sarah Louise Magee (13)
Our Lady Of Mercy Secondary School

HALLOWE'EN

Fireworks explode in the night,
Cats and dogs run in fright,
The full moon shines in the sky
As the wicked witch goes flying by.

The little children go trick or treat,
For candy apples and nuts to eat,
Dressed as vampires and scary spooks,
Causing strange and frightened looks.

Later when the fun and parties stop
Kids are tired and ready to drop,
Lying in the dark in bed,
They cannot sleep thinking of the dead.

Mary-Beth Fennell (13)
Our Lady Of Mercy Secondary School

HALLOWE'EN IS HERE

Hallowe'en is here again
time for fun and games to play
duck for apples, crack some nuts
stuff our faces, greedy guts.

Fireworks crack, bang and fizz
rockets light the sky so bright
monsters jumping from dark holes
skeletons, devils and scary ghouls.

Witches flying on rickety brooms,
with all speed back to their tombs.
I will never get to sleep tonight
afraid of a horrible evil sight.

Caoimhe O'Donnell (13)
Our Lady Of Mercy Secondary School

SPOOKY, SPECTACULAR SIGHTS

Fireworks flutter
Fairies fly
Up, up high in the sky.

Weary, witches
Wondering wild
Looking for children
As they fly.

Ghosts popping up
Here and there,
While the children
Are running a scare.

At the stroke of midnight
The children
Are out of sight.

All the parents give
A cheer, because they
Know Hallowe'en is
Over for another year.

Sarah McLarnon (13)
Our Lady Of Mercy Secondary School

Hallowe'en

Witches, ghosts and goblins are out and about
It's time for trick or treat.
Fireworks, candy apples and parties.

Time for carving pumpkins,
Children waving sparklers in the
All Hallows Eve wind.
The one night of the year when the dead can
Return to earth.

Watch out you might be in for a fright.
Sleep tight.

Martine Magee (14)
Our Lady Of Mercy Secondary School

Hallowe'en Night

At 12.00 o'clock on Hallowe'en night,
If you're still out you'll get a fright.
There are ghosts, goblins and witches too,
All running about and shouting boo!

If you're not brave but wanna try,
Don't go out when they're passing by.
The might hit you with sticks,
They might hit you with stones,
The skeleton might even hit you with bones.

So after 12.00 o'clock on Hallowe'en night
Don't go out or you'll get a big fright!

Christine Murphy (13)
Our Lady Of Mercy Secondary School

MY PENCIL

My pencil's called Jim
You must understand
And his favourite place is the palm of my hand.

He's made out of wood
With a big pointy head
And his favourite colours are green, black and red.

Jim's just a pencil
And has not a brain
When put through the sharpener, he doesn't feel pain.

I sometimes am cruel
And more often kind
But sometimes I chew him and bite his behind.

In a case made for pencils
Found not far from here
Jim plays cards with his friends and then has a beer.

I can't write anymore.
I hope you won't pout
But Jim is not quite well and soon will run out.

My sharpener's lost
And that is my strife
There is only one option not nice.

I could sharpen Jim
But it would be a sin
To carve him up using a knife.

Geraldine Boyle (13)
St Dominic's High School

My Neighbourhood

The large trees sway in the wind,
The leaves fall upon the ground,
All is quiet.

But when winter comes,
Things are different,
It's cold and icy.

When spring arrives,
Flowers bloom,
Trees regain their colour.

Then comes summer!
It's warm and fun for everyone,
Children come out and play.

At night it is very quiet and dark,
Until you hear a dog bark,
The children are all in bed asleep
And from the houses there is not a peep,
The moon shines upon the road
And there is no sign of Mr Toad
In my neighbourhood.

Bernadette McQuillan (13)
St Dominic's High School

The Seasons

Spring is the season when the flowers grow and lambs are born,
The farmers harvest their corn,
This marks a new beginning.

Summer is the season of holidays and fun,
The beaches are full of people
Soaking up the sun.

Autumn is the season when all the leaves turn brown,
They fall off the trees,
Onto the ground.

Winter is the season when snow begins to fall,
Christmas carols are sung,
By one and all.

Noirin Kearney (13)
St Dominic's High School

MY FAVOURITE HOBBIES

I want to talk to you about the way I feel,
When I'm on the stage and I'm doing a reel
It feels so right it can't be wrong,
Especially when I've been doing it for so long.
I've been dancing from four to fourteen,
You'd think I'd be tired, but I've had a few breaks in between.
Dancing is part of our culture and character,
The Irish people will dance come hell or high water,
It can break down barriers and make strangers friends,
Of this we should be proud, let's hope it never ends.
When I dance I dress up and wear nice shoes,
You should hear my beats treble ones, treble twos.
Riverdance brought us to the world-wide stage,
So now if you're good at dancing you can earn a wage.
Hopefully within the next few years, I'll have the chance,
To be one of the stars in Lord of the Dance.
My name in the programme you will see,
Lord of the Dance starring Roisin McIlduff and Michael Flatley
And if I don't get that far, it won't matter really,
'Cause I can still strut my stuff down at the local ceili.

Roisin McIlduff (14)
St Dominic's High School

ART

They say that to draw
You have to be good at art
But just grab a pencil
And draw from your heart.

It takes a little practice
but in no time at all
whether bottles or people
you will be able to draw.

Take an object
a hat, bag or shoe
and put it on a table
straight in front of you.

You don't need oil pastels
or fancy coloured paints
just use a pencil
and it will turn out great.

You start at the bottom
and work your way to the top
and once you have started
you won't want to stop.

Drawing is easy
no matter what people say
and you don't have to wait till

Art class

you can draw any day.

**Úna Méabh Herron (13)
St Dominic's High School**

THE WINTER SNOW

In the winter while it's cold
Children are playing and being bold
Throwing snowballs all around
Making angels on the ground.

Not me - oh no!
I don't play in that snow
I just stay in and watch TV
Why can't they all be good like me?

A big round head
And a fat belly too
They make it from snow
That's what they do!
A carrot for a nose
A button for an eye
Why can't they be good?
Why? Why? Why?

The sun comes out
The snow melts,
All the children cry
I have to ask myself again
Why aren't they good?
Why?

Katrina Brennan (13)
St Dominic's High School

A New Beginning

It was once a small bulb,
Planted in the soil,
Adding a little water, it soon began to sprout.
Leaves began to develop,
Pure green straining at the veins with life.
Buds begin to burst forth,
From their comfortable layers,
Because of a sun shining bright.

The buds like any grew,
And opened slowly.
To produce a beauteous flower,
Colourful, scented, delicate,
But tall and upright.

Winter covers the country,
Turning the weather cold,
The flower feels the pinch,
And slowly life ebbs away,
No more a feast of grandeur to meet the eye.

Winter's end, flowers drift,
In the breeze crumpled and crisp they blow.
A dreary landscape left so bare,
Devoid of splendour.

And then, with the first spring ray of light,
It will explode in colour,
As bulbs begin the cycle again.

Our lives can be like the bulb,
Let bad things crumple and die,
Let new ideas burst forth,
And face a new millennium with hope.

Pauline Gough (14)
St Dominic's High School

DID YOU KNOW?

Daddy! Daddy! Did you know
That pigs cannot swim in snow?
Did you hear that fish have ears
And that granny likes a quiet beer?

Daddy! Guess what? Have you seen
The ants that like to eat washing machines?
Daddy! Did you ever notice
How Aunt Ethel's hair is full of locusts?

Daddy! Tell me did you meet
That cross old man from down the street?
Daddy! I wonder have you seen
His head as shiny as our TV screen?

Daddy! You know what? I think he grows
Rhubarb and custard up in his nose!

Daddy! Granny says you'd never believe
How his wife has threatened to leave
I heard Uncle say they should put him away
He could stay in my box where I put toys to stay.

Daddy! Did . . . ahh That's quite enough dear
Why don't you play with your toys over here?
You see, daddy has lots of hard word to do
So go and play nurse . . . Look! Dolly has flu!

But Daddy that's what you *always* say
When mum's not here and gran's away
You say you have lots of work to do
But you lie on the sofa and comfortably snooze!

Oonagh Barronwell (13)
St Dominic's High School

THE MILLENNIUM BUG

What exactly is this Millennium Bug?
When people ask me all I can do is shrug.
But then one day when I was asleep in my bed
This funny little creature appeared in my head.
It had lots of legs and was covered in spots
Wide wings, round eyes and feelers on top.
I walked up to him and gave him a tug
'Who are you?' I asked. 'I'm the Millennium Bug.'
We were introduced and soon became friends
So I said 'What will happen when this year ends?'
'Oh me, I'm afraid I will be such a pest
Breaking down computers, TV's and all the rest
I do not mean to cause all this trouble
But I'll have to commence when those zeros do double
As my mind does not understand this new start
I'll unfortunately have to tear these items apart
I've heard some objects have been treated against me
So they will not be affected, but I will not flee!
Now I've warned you well and now I must leave
So be well prepared this New Years Eve!'

Karen Molloy (13)
St Dominic's High School

THE MILLENNIUM BUG

The Millennium Bug is coming,
It's bite is short and sharp and sweet.
As it is in that split second when you'll
Hear your computer go beep.

The Millennium Bug is coming
And it has a cunning plan.
It wants to ruin every old computer
In the whole of this land.

The Millennium Bug is coming,
And everyone may be aware.
Because on New Years Eve,
If you don't have a good trick
Up your sleeve,
You'll soon be aware of what's coming.

Paula Kearney (14)
St Dominic's High School

THE LOSS OF A FRIEND

Before you went I never knew
How much you meant to me.
But now you're gone, I realise
The love that we once shared.
I should have cherished every moment
Not realising that some day you'd be gone.

You left me early in your life
To be somewhere close to God.
You're up among the deep blue sky
At night you are a shining star.

There' much in life you did not experience,
And still had to achieve.
You never complained about your illness,
But carried on the best you could.

You were a strong, determined person
Whom I greatly admire.
You are thought of every day,
And remembered in a special way.
- You will never be forgotten.

Mary Moran (15)
St Dominic's High School

NATURE'S WAY

Every raindrop that falls from the sky,
Every tear drop that falls from my eye
Every flower that buds in May,
Everything I do or say.

Every sea with its fish and coral,
Every happiness, every sorrow
Every song a bluebird sings
Every event a new day brings.

Every beat from a heart,
Every ending, every start
Every risk, every dare,
Every lifetime that we share.

Flowers, bird, animals, trees,
From the highest peaks to the deepest seas
God created it all for us,
So thank Him and praise Him.

This poem was written to say,
Everything in every possible way
About our world and who we are,
Nature's special something for all of us to share!

Karen McIlvenny (13)
St Dominic's High School

The Autumn Season

The changing seasons come and go
The trees and flowers lose all their glow.

The summer is slipping far away
The nights creep in and shorten each day.

The garden is tidied
The tubs are stripped
All the colour is gone and the flowers are nipped.

Bulbs hang, hoping for some sunlight
No warmth,
No heat,
They creep out of sight.

How sad this time looks each year
Until the colours, once again.
Creep in offering cheer.

The yellows and russets spread out like a spray
Giving nature some hope for a brighter day.

Autumn moves it won't stand and wait
Like humans and animals it accepts its fate.

From green for growth to a dying brown
Autumn will touch all around.

Claire Rooney (14)
St Dominic's High School

WATER'S SONG

I am the waves which pound the cliffs
And wear away the stone.
I am the waves which crash against the rocks
In the fury of the storm.
I am the waves lapping along the shore
Pulling gently at the sand.
I am the clear, cold river
Rushing down the glen.
I am the gurgling spring, high on the windy mountain.
I am the muddy farmyard pond,
The rain which falls from the sky
I am the green and murky lough
Hiding strange creatures in my depths
I seep under the ground, through the soil
To feed the new young plants.
I quench your thirst in the dry sandy desert,
Beneath the scorching sun.
I was here at the beginning of time.
I am water, giving life to all things.

Ita Monaghan (12)
St Dominic's High School

FASHION

Some people like to wear black
Some people like white
Some people like to wear them loose
Some people like them tight.

Fancy trousers, fancy tops
My mummy thinks it's over the top
Miss Selfridges, New Look, International
Without them all it would be hell.

Buying make-up is a must,
But using other people's I don't trust.
As cold sores are quite contagious
And getting them away takes ages.

Fashion is everywhere
Wear it if you dare
Some people just don't
Some people won't.

Clara McCurdy (13)
St Dominic's High School

STARLIGHT, STARBRIGHT

Star of the night,
Twinkles so bright,
Like the eyes of a tiger cat,
Shining in the light.

Like a flame in the sky,
I often wonder why?
You don't blow out
When I swiftly pass by.

You watch over the land,
Everything goes as planed,
When you leave the night sky,
With the moon hand in hand.

Soon you are here,
We're not afraid, no fear!
As you light our way through the dark.
We are comforted when you are near.

Clare Galway (12)
St Dominic's High School

I Sometimes Wonder Why?

Why am I me,
Why are you, you
Why do we do the things that we do,
Why does the moon come out at night,
Why do brothers and sisters fight?

Are all teachers afraid to be nice,
Why are we afraid of mice,
Why do Chinese people mostly eat rice,
And why is the world unkind and not nice,
Is it because they never think twice?

Why is the winter cold,
Why is the summer warm,
Why does the winter seem long,
And why does the summer seem short?
All these answers I do not know,
But I hope someday that the answers will show.

Kathy Crawford (12)
St Dominic's High School

A Winter's Day

As the snowflakes fall gently on the ground,
And as the bare trees whistle in the wind,
The sky clouds over with snow-driven clouds,
And everything is dusted with snowflakes.

The morning has arrived,
And everything is cold and frozen,
I look out of my window and see the birds
on the dusted branches of the tree.

Now it is afternoon,
And everything is back to normal.
Watching it all melt away during the day,
Snowmen slowly melting away into the ground,
That was our winter, it only lasted twenty-four hours.

Helen Brady (14)
St Dominic's High School

MUSIC

There are lots of different types of music
Pop, rock, jazz and dance too
Different people have different tastes
Just like me and you.

I like most kinds of music
Like Nirvana, Oasis and Boyzone too,
Backstreet Boys, Stereophonics and Five
To name but a few.

The music played by all these groups
Have different words and different tunes
They keep their individuality
Until their time is through.

All newspapers and reporters lie
About their private lives
But if you are a real true fan
You'll never criticise.

Without their talent
You would be bored
So buy their singles
Even those you can hardly afford.

Sarah McGlinchey (13)
St Dominic's High School

THE WOODS

The birds play on the wall
I wonder if they ever fall?
A far-off call in the woods,
The woods,
Full of fear!
What's near?
A rat, a squirrel
A cracking log.
Maybe it's just my ears
But take heed of what
Might just lurk between
The trees.
That cries out in misery
On every Hallowe'en night
There comes an eerie glow
At Christmas time there are
Footprints in the snow.
They say that the woods
Are haunted.
But I never go near
The birds play on the wall
I wonder if they ever fall?
A far-off call in the woods,
The woods like a maze
Full of fear
What's near?
I don't go here.

Sorcha Eastwood (14)
St Dominic's High School

WISE KINGS

Wise kings, three in a row
With presents glistening and tied with a bow
Following a star that twinkled upon the night,
So bright, so bright it was always in sight.
As the journey continues they stop to see
A little barn where he could be
Lucky enough he is there,
Everyone's here but he doesn't care.
The donkeys, the sheep, the calf are there
His father created land, sea and air.
But don't forget most of all,
He's Christ our Saviour, King of all.

Siobhán Gibson (14)
St Dominic's High School

MORNING

I wake up to find my alarm clock ringing,
The sweet sound of the blackbirds singing,
Then I arise,
Wipe the sleep out of my eyes,
Downstairs to where my uniform's pressed,
Then back upstairs, where I get dressed
Go into the kitchen where there's something
To munch,
Then I grab my blazer, school bag as
Well as my lunch.
Must run, can't be late,
Bus arrives at twenty to eight.

Roisin Walsh (14)
St Dominic's High School

KITTENS

As I look out my window
At the leaves falling from the trees
Brown and crispy.
Black puffs of fluff
Pounce on each one
As they fall to the ground.
As I look at them now
Remembering how they
Huddled in their mother's fur
Small and blind.
Now, as I look at them
Big and strong
Ready to face the world.

Kathleen Healey (14)
St Dominic's High School

WHAT IS A BOOK?

A book is a bar of chocolate waiting to be eaten.
As we unravel the paper we explore new things,
Like turning the pages in a book.
The bright colours on the wrapper are very inviting,
Like the blurb on the back of a novel
As we read the text new themes are encountered,
Like flavours in the chocolate
As the book now comes to a conclusion,
Or as the chocolate is consumed down to the last bite,
All we wish for is to experience it all over again.

Sinéad Burns (14)
St Dominic's High School

TWEETY PIE

Tweety Pie is cute and yellow,
He is a charming little fellow.
He likes to love everyone,
Bugs, Daffy, Taz and him are always having fun.
But they don't let Sylvester join in because he is a
Sneaky guy.
He doesn't like that yellow little bird he always wants
Him to die.
To get him he always tries tricks,
But Granny finds out and gives him a kick.
Tweety can be anything he wants to be,
Robin Hood, Prince Charming or even you.
Why do we love Tweety so much?
Because he is cute, sweet and soft to touch.

Lyndsay Meredith (14)
St Dominic's High School

31ST OCTOBER

Children dress up to go
Trick or treating.
Pumpkins glow in the dark.
Ghosts and ghouls look at you everywhere.
Wizards and witches cast a terrible spell.
Spiders, beetles, cockroaches too,
Crawl all over you.
Vampires suck on your blood
To stay alive while they leave you to die.
The dark has gone and day is alive
All is left for another year.

Katie McGarry (13)
St Dominic's High School

FRIENDSHIP

Our time together was wonderful,
for we stuck to each other like glue,
even when we shouldn't have,
that was the time we both had flu.
There were times we had some quarrels,
but they never lasted long,
for you only had to smile at me and that quarrel was long-gone.
The day I have always dreaded, when you travelled far away.
Your family went to Australia and you did not have a say.
It really made a difference as the hurt was very deep,
Most nights I'd go to bed and cry myself to sleep.
Then the letters started coming almost every day,
to tell me all the news about Australia far away.
I felt no happiness once again, I knew you felt that too,
but the happiness did not last for long,
when I heard no news from you.
Months passed by without a word, I felt this awful pain,
I prayed to God to let me know and to take away this pain.
Now my prayers were answered, even though my news was sad,
I thank you God for everything and the good friend that I had.
So if you have a friend, tell them that you care, for you may not get another chance.
When they are no longer there.

Sarah Mc Caul (14)
St Dominic's High School

WHAT IF?

What would one be,
If one hadn't any life.
What would be a butcher,
If a butcher had no knife?

What would be a picture,
If the picture had no colour?
What would be a sister,
If a sister had no brother?

What would be a light bulb,
If that light bulb had no light?
What would be a boxer,
If a boxer could not fight?

What would be an artist,
If an artist couldn't draw?
What would be a lawyer,
If there wasn't any law?

What would be bread,
If there wasn't any crust?
What would be a friend,
If in your friend, you could not trust?

What would be a rainbow,
If there wasn't any gold?
What would be the winter,
If we could not feel the cold?

What would we do,
If everyone asked questions?

Sarah O'Connell (14)
St Dominic's High School

SHOPPING TRIP

Finally she turned up.
Racing down the aisles,
We arrived at the shop
And we were in our 'clothes heaven'.

Tracing our hands over
All the fabrics,
Velvet, velour, cotton, silk,
And nearly blinded

By all the beautiful colours.
What fun we had trying on
All the clothes and
Seeing which one suited

Us best. It had to be the
Black trousers and blue top for me,
While Lisa went for the pretty pink.

Skirt and purple blouse. As
we queued to pay for the clothes,
We began to think of what shoes to buy.

Now that was another story!

Emer Denny (14)
St Dominic's High School

A Time Of Year

Christmas is my favourite day,
When Santa comes on his sleigh.
What guides his sleigh is eight tiny reindeer,
That make a soft noise when they come near.
He has a round face and a big round belly,
That wobbles when he laughs, like a plateful of jelly.
He only comes once a year at night,
When everybody's in bed and out of sight.
He brings the boys and girls a toy,
Which makes them happy and full of joy.
Their stockings get hung on the fireplace with care,
While the children all hope that he'll soon be there.
Then they all go and snuggle up in their beds,
With the thought of Santa still in their heads.

Eva Dugan (15)
St Dominic's High School

Have You Ever Wondered . . . ?

What was here before the world began?
Was everything just silent?
With no one to judge the human race,
And no one to be violent?
Was God the only one about,
Is that why he made man?
Well, if he did, it all worked out,
This great big master plan.
If God exists, then who made God?
Was he just always there?
And if he just stays in heaven
Then where is heaven . . . where?

Bronagh Diamond (12)
St Dominic's High School

WONDERS OF THE WORLD

How was this world invented,
And how did we come about,
And how did all the people learn,
To talk and scream and shout?

How did God get on Earth,
To show us all the way,
And why do people have to die,
Is it on Earth we cannot stay?

What was here before the world,
Was it just a dark, dark sky,
And who named all the objects,
And for what reason why?

How did the first tree grow,
And all the flowers and plants,
And who named all the insects,
All the spiders and the ants?

Who invented everything,
And how do birds so softly sing,
How did anything ever come about?
These are the things, I think about.

Clare Hilland (12)
St Dominic's High School

Television

I watch it every day and night,
It fills my day with such delight,
To watch it brings me so much joy,
And to every other girl and boy.

My parents think that it's a pain,
But why they do, I can't explain?
There's lots of things that you can watch,
From cartoons to a football match!

If you've got cable you're doing great,
You're gotta watch number thirty-eight,
It's the music channel it's the best,
It's far better than the rest.

For short we call it TV,
It's something to watch for you and me,
I love it so much I kiss it goodnight,
It's my friend and is always right!

Clíodhna Massey (12)
St Dominic's High School

Apple And Blackcurrant Pie

First bit is crunchy and crispy
you hear the crackle in your mouth
sweet slabs of blackcurrant
the apple sour and syrupy
bursting with bitterness
flaky and soft as snowflakes
apple and blackcurrant pie!

Bronagh Clarke (12)
St Rose's High School

FAMILIES

Families are sacred and always there for you
For you, your brothers and your sisters too.
When you're sad and even when you're happy
They have been there from when you were in a nappy.

Family life is happy but sometimes sad
They can even make you mad
With their shouting and groaning
Someone's always moaning.

My mum always says family is special
And that we all need them.
I agree with her and believe the same
I believe we need them and without them we would be lonely.

I believe they are a part of everyday life
To help to take away some of the strife.
To share and to be kind
And they're not just in your mind.

They are real and we need them so much
To love, caress and to touch.
To show how much they love you
And how much you love them.

Always remember you need them
And they need you,
For advice, love and understanding too
Families are special and that means you.

Lyndsey Murray (15)
St Rose's High School

FRIENDS

Your friends are the closest thing in the world to you,
They're your buddies, your chums, your companions.

Some may be closer to you than others,
And some you may share your most inner secrets with.
These are the one you trust and confide in,
The ones that know everything about you.
The ones that are true.

You also have friends who back-stab or criticise the others,
The ones who believe they're big and above the rest,
The ones in charge that everyone listens to,
The type everyone else is afraid of,
And wouldn't even think of talking back to.
These ones are hardly friends, but more like bullies or rivals.

Friends are of different sorts,
Kind, mean, good, bad,
But you'll always have the ones you hate,
And the ones you love.
You may also have the ones you just like too.
But in spite of all our differences,
We may someday soon,
Become friends that are real, honest and true.

Seáneen Mallon (15)
St Rose's High School

DARK MEMORIES

Crash!
I heard a scream, then silence.
She lay there so still,
No one knew what had happened.

We all ran over,
There was a tiny cut on her forehead,
Droplets of blood were trickling down her pale face.

A crowd began to gather,
Some of them were crying, shocked, questioning
each other, the rest went to find help.

The girl was about seven or eight,
Fair hair, pale skinned,
Dressed in white, like an angel.

An ambulance arrived,
Took her away,
Another life taken, but no one to pay.

Bronagh McGlinchey (15)
St Rose's High School

BULLY BADNESS

Bullies are cruel, nasty and mean,
They pick on people over the slightest thing,
You cannot hide for they will seek,
They pick on people who are weak.

Most are cowards, they hang with a crowd,
They're really abusive and often loud,
They will not confront when they're alone
They need their gang to taunt and stone.

Bullies are jealous, they often say
'You're not popular so go away.'
But a bully can only keep you weak,
If you do not, stand up and speak.

So if a bully you do meet,
Don't back down, stand on your feet,
But if you can't, then look around,
There's always help to be found.

Colleen Brady (12)
St Rose's High School

FORMAL DAY

On Friday at three
We hear a shout
Because school is out
Everyone feels free.

The bathroom is being used
For a make-up studio
As my sister sings 'Here we go.'

It's only 6 o'clock
The dinner isn't till nine
She keeps on saying
'I'll be fine.'

Her formal date awaits
In his house already dressed
In case he is late.

8 o'clock comes and they are ready
Off they go together
Like a husband and wife.

Catherine Rock (15)
St Rose's High School

Better Than Anyone Else

My mum whom I love so much
The person I love to touch.
She brightens up my dullest days
Oh how I love her friendly touch.

She's my best friend
To whom I trust.
Even though I don't show it much
She knows I love her, oh so much.

She's smart and fun
And would do anything for anyone.
Sometimes she's too nice
Doing too much for everyone.

If she were to go
I wouldn't know what to do.
I'd miss her, oh so much
My best friend, the one I trust.

Never would I forget her
Nor would anyone else.
For she's one in a million
Better than anyone, anywhere else.

Joanne Donnelly (14)
St Rose's High School

MY GRANDAD DENIS

How I wish I could see you
Just us eye to eye.
I wish I could hug you tight
Like my granny does every night.

I was your first grandchild
You never got to see.
Because you died so suddenly
Everyone saying what a good man you were
And how you used to style your hair.

I visit your grave and bring you
prayers and flowers.
I look below, I look above
Trying to see your shining love.

God took you up to his wondrous place
and if he didn't.
I would find the spaces in my heart
I know I could make a whole new start.

I wish I could have seen his beautiful face
Shining down from his wonderful place.
One day we will be together forever,
Without a care in the world.

Denise Keatings (14)
St Rose's High School

A Fantasy Land

In a made-up land
far, far away
Dreams are reality
and everything comes true.

Smiley faces fill the land
and happy cries fill the air.
Everyone cheerful not a tear in sight
cos this is the night
not to be filled with fright.

Wishes come true
there is no school
and we can stay up
as late as we like.

If only this was real
and think what fun it would be.
To have everything around me
that I have ever wanted.
Oh it's such a dream
unfortunately not real!

Claire Carson (14)
St Rose's High School

Seasons

Seasons are such glorious things
Each one has a different light that it brings
Spring summer autumn and winter too
They show us the world is turning you know that it's true

The seasons never age you see
So the question is why do we?

The seasons stay forever young
They do not age in the burning sun,
Or the snow the sleet or rain
They repeat their beauty all over again

While we age and fade away
We know that the beauty of the seasons will stay.

Katrina Connolly (14)
St Rose's High School

MY MEMORIES OF MY GRANNY

When I think of your smiling face
It brings back memories of how we were
Of the good times I spent with you
And how we did everything together

I think of when we would shop the day away
And how much time I spent with you
I think of how it used to be
And how it will never be the same without you

You were taken away from me
And now I'm left with a space in my heart
Thinking of how much I loved you
And wishing you would come back to me

Now you're gone and memories
Are all I have to remember you
I wish each day you would come back
Into my life and fill my heart
But now you're gone and I only have memories.

Kaleena Morelli (14)
St Rose's High School

FUNDERLAND

As I waited in the queue
I feared for my own life
Because I heard loud voices
Screaming out for help.

My knees began to shake
And my face turned white.
My head started to spin
This didn't feel right.

When I got inside
There was many things to do.
Small rides for children
And big ones for me and you.

Ones that went upside-down
Plain ones that went round.
I wanted to be brave
But, my feet stayed on the ground.

I got on the small roller-coaster
With children half my age.
I couldn't face the ghost train
My friends were full of rage.

They kept giving me weird looks
I couldn't understand why.
Well, I was having fun
I feel so happy now.

I was sad to see it go
Because I had a great time.
I want to go back next year
Maybe then I'll feel fine.

Deborah O'Neill (14)
St Rose's High School

MATHEMATICS

Don't laugh . . . maths is fun!

Maths is very exciting
Adding, multiplying and dividing
If you get one wrong
You just keep on trying.

I think adding is my favourite
Because they're easy to do
21 + 21
Of course makes 42.

My class is good at maths
They learn tables in a day
But I know someone who doesn't care
And just goes out to play.

Mrs Rafferty is happy if you
Get them all right
She says, 'Very good'
Being very polite.

I bet you think I'm boasting
Because I said I know what to do
But remember in the poem
I said something about you . . .

Antoinette Smith (11)
St Rose's High School

MY FAMILY AND I

I love my family from the bottom of my heart
And one thing's for sure,
We are never far apart.

We depend on one another,
When things go wrong,
For we all know
There's one of us who is always strong.

We have our ups and downs,
Our fall outs too
But we can honestly say
At the end of the day
Everything turns out to be just OK.

My family are my mum and dad,
Two sisters, three brothers are what I have
Our house is always noisy
I'm sure you'll understand,
Every one of us are always in demand.

My mum and dad I have to thank
For the love and patience they have towards us all,
I can honestly say at the end of the day
They have shown us their love in every special way.

Well I have wrote about my family
I am proud as can be that we build
That love together
Just like a family tree.

Charlene Barkley (13)
St Rose's High School

CHRISTMAS

As the nights get darker and the days colder,
Winter is approaching us
Magical stars twinkle in the nightly sky
And children wait in anticipation
For Christmas day is getting closer.

With the darkness of night comes a magical touch,
For Christmas is getting closer.

They hope for snow to fall from the sky,
To cover each street in a thick coat of white
As the sight of it was bewitching.

Christmas day has finally arrived,
All the excitement is no longer contained in children,
It floats freely from them.
A new emotion, fascination, takes over
Caused by presents they have been given
And the glorious day ahead.
Parents watch, with satisfaction,
The happiness in their children's eyes.

Everyone is buzzing with energy.
The atmosphere is entrancing,
But they have pushed aside
The real meaning of Christmas,
Our Lord's birthday.

Yolanda Cox (14)
St Rose's High School

Autumn

Swaying in the breeze,
From side to side
The leaves float then fall
The colours - red, brown, yellow
Land all around
I watch to see the trees grow empty

Soon the leaves are gone
And the trees lie bare
The branches, lonely and cold
All that can be heard,
Is the sound of the wind
And all that can be seen
Is the movement of the trees

It is quiet now
With no one around
The ground can't be seen
And the trees lie bare
The colours - red, brown, yellow
So still.

Deirdre Melly (14)
St Rose's High School

My Granny

Open close, open close,
I sat beside her beside holding her hand.
I watched her eyes open and close.

It was autumn, her favourite time of year,
We would usually go out and walk through the leaves.
It won't happen again I fear.

The great stories we shared together.
I wish I could make her stay.
But her eyes have closed, she looks at peace.
I'll meet her another day.

Claire Agnew (12)
St Rose's High School

LONGEST FIVE MINUTES

Five minutes to go
Hurry up and come
Watching the clock
It takes forever
As the second hand goes around
It gets slower and slower
Tick tock tick tock

The sounds are annoying
The scratching of pens
The scuffling of books
The whispering of the other impatient girls
But the others the patient girls just sit there
And think and stare

Then I feel a tap on my shoulder
A familiar but soft voice asks
'Do you have the time?'
And as she got to the last word the bell rang.

At last Friday afternoon and it is five past three
for the next two days no school at all.

Louise McKenna (12)
St Rose's High School

LONELINESS STRIKES

Standing in the courtyard
So lonely, so down.
Waiting on someone
To ask me to join their game.
I'm still waiting
Cold am I
Someone oh someone help me
Oh no they are coming towards me
The group of God knows who
'Hi do you want to play?'
Yes of course I would
Love to play with you
We'll play
A game of tippy you, you, and you
Stand here beside me
I am so free.

Lena Buttimer (12)
St Rose's High School

THE DRAKE

On a cold winter's mornin'
In the middle of November
Everywhere was frozen,
Across the lake
Went the blue scooting duck.

Its black feathered wings
Rested nicely on its rounded body
Its beak the usual orange
With ice nicely perked on top.

As the drake lead the path
And the ducklings followed
It left a trail on the ice
Swerving right and left
As the dawn broke through.

Laura Osborne (13)
St Rose's High School

THE BIG DAY

It's eight o'clock just thirty minutes more
Until my friends call at my door.
We walk into school
I see that everyone is looking at me!

I find a seat beside my friend
I'm hoping that day will end
The teachers come we raise to our feet
Wonder what friends I'll meet?

Butterflies in my tummy
Oh my God I want my mummy
We went with the teacher
She was awfully nice
My fears had died
My happiness had arrived

I met a new friend
Her name was Natasha
I stayed with her all day
Until the day had drifted away.

Lindsey McVarnock (12)
St Rose's High School

MY LITTLE DOLL

My doll comes to life
At night.
She wakes up and jumps
Off the shelf.
She looks around the room
Bump, bump through the night.
No one around, apart
From my little red doll.
She wakes the other dolls
They play all night.
You can't hear a thing
Apart from their little feet
Going round and round
Bump, bump through the night.

Lindsay Mullan (12)
St Rose's High School

PASSION FRUITS

Plum pickers pack plums perfectly
Strawberries spotted skin smells sweetly
Melons might make Maisie's muesli
Grapes grow greater green gracefully
Blackberries blossom black buds beautifully
Banana boats bring back bananas brightly
Apricots almost always act accordingly
Lemons like lying low lazily.

Ciara Leathem (12)
St Rose's High School

I Just Can't Resist

When a chocolate cake is sitting right in
front of you, you talk about it.
You start to feel hunger
and your temptation is bursting
Cloying as cocoa
Amazing
Amusing
Velvety
Cushiony
Sun-kissed
Chocolatey delicious
Tempting
The cake is bottomless
From largeness to darkness
Sweetened and flavoursome.

Stephanie McCann (12)
St Rose's High School

The Moon

A planet whiter
Than any other
Round but smaller
Than Jupiter
It is brighter
Than a lighter
Makes life happier
And will forever.

Katrina Morgan (12)
St Rose's High School

HALLOWE'EN NIGHT

On Hallowe'en night
The witches come out
The ghosts come out too
We all get a fright

We dress up to scare things
We go trick or treat
Babies are crying
Ready to scream
On Hallowe'en night which gives us a fright

We're shouting 'Boo!'
And singing songs
We are happy
And our parents are too

Hallowe'en scares wee babies
Ghosts are everywhere
Everywhere is black
We are sad when Hallowe'en is over
Hallowe'en night will give us a *fright.*

Donna Marie Rock (11)
St Rose's High School

COMING TOGETHER

Peace we want
And peace there will be
Peace for people like
You and me

To walk down the street
Forbidden one time
To talk to people
Once enemies of mine

To run and play
without fear of a gun
To run and play
All we want is some fun!

To grow up with people
Without bullets or bombs
To grow up with people
Where one God rules us all.

Francine Milnes (11)
St Rose's High School

HALLOWE'EN

Hallowe'en is a scary day,
People come out to play,
They sing songs,
They dance, they cry
They pray to God
Oh my, oh my

You don't know where they are,
Because they're all covered up in hair,
You don't see their faces
And other places,

All the bangers
Go up in the air,
And scare people everywhere,

So that is the night,
When people get such a bad
                    Fright!

Susanna Toner (11)
St Rose's High School

CATS

Our house is full of cats
Or so it seems
We have three
Two sit on the ceiling beams
And the other one sleeps all day
On Dad's favourite chair
When Dad's not there.

One is called Phil
And the other is Lil
And the third is named Bill
We adore our cats
So please Mrs Sewell
Don't be cruel
To our cats.

Hannah Donnelly (11)
St Rose's High School

MONEY

Money, money is fun to spend
Better when you're with a friend
My friend and I would spend all day
I can't wait till I get my pay

Wonder how much I'll spend
I will buy things in tens
I might buy a few pens
Wonder when?

I might go to Funderland
Where will I stand?
It will cost a lot of money
But hey so what buddy.

Emma Brady (11)
St Rose's High School

MY PET HAMSTER!

My pet hamster is fat and furry
That's why I call him Furby
I love to sit and watch him eat
I always give him a nice treat
I used to let him run about the house
But people got frightened
And thought he was a mouse
He plays on his wheel
All night long
And he doesn't stop till the break of dawn
His fur is brown and white
He keeps me up all night
I love him very much
But I can't stand his touch
He is very special to me
He fills me up with glee
He is such a special thing
We treat him as if he is a king
We hope he will stay forever more
For he is the pet that we adore.

Margarette Shortt (11)
St Rose's High School

LEAVES

I look out my back window
And what can I see?
Clish clash on the ground
Leaves falling off a tree
They're brown they're hard
They're easy to squash
Clish clash clish clash.

It starts to rain,
Everybody's running home
You can hear the squash squash
On the leaves, crunch crunch
On the leaves squashing and
Splashing on the ground,
Can't you hear all the sound?

Patricia Taggart (11)
St Rose's High School

AUTUMN IS HERE

Autumn time is here
We scream, we shout, we cheer,
The leaves are falling down
On the hard, hard ground.

I love the sound of the leaves
Falling down onto my hands
And onto the ground
Crunch, crunch and crunch, crunch, crunch, crunch.

I stamp on the leaves
Until they all blow away
I feel sad there is
No game to play.

Aisling Kelly (11)
St Rose's High School

EVERY DAY DESIRING YOU

My love is like a piece of gold,
Hard to get and hard to hold.
But now that you have stolen my heart
It's a shame we are so far apart.

Even though you used me badly
I have forgiven you ever so gladly.
The love that burns inside my heart
Is stronger now that we are far apart.

Words cannot describe what I have to say
Please don't cast my heart astray.
My heart yearns for you every day
Now and until my dying day.

My heart is faithful and true to you
Oh please say you love me too!
And your heart will always be true
If not, why? What did I do?

I close my eyes and I still see you there
With your hands caressing my long brown hair.
Because you know my heart will always be true
Every day desiring you.

Francine Jack (14)
St Rose's High School

Autumn Time

As it comes into autumn,
All the leaves fall to the ground,
As we walk through the park,
Crunch, crunch, as we stand on the crispy brown leaves.

All hats, scarves and gloves on,
As we enter autumn,
Red noses, cold ears,
Running noses, chesty coughs and sore throats.

Cold days, cold nights,
It's time to wear trousers and tights,
Not shorts and ankle socks.

Claire Marie Kerr (11)
St Rose's High School

Hallowe'en

Trick or treater
Sweet eater
Witch dresser
Door rapper
Horror watcher
Scream lover
Story teller.

Thomasina Lindsay (11)
St Rose's High School

My Monkey

Brown, petite with an extended tail
Clinging hands which hold you tight
A bumper face
Two tiny brown ears
Two large eyes
A little mouth with a little tooth
A small black nose
Sitting on chubby legs
On my oblong shelf just above my bed
Guiding and watching over me
As I call her my lucky charm.

Letitia Mulgrave (11)
St Rose's High School

Autumn

Autumn brings coughs and colds
Using tissues to blow my nose
The trees are sneezing
Their leaves to the ground
Green to red, orange and brown
The nights seem longer
The streets get darker
The moon gets brighter
The air gets colder
For autumn will be here next year.

Orlaith Malocco (11)
St Rose's High School

Hallowe'en

Hallowe'en is coming,
Hallowe'en is near,
It is scary
And Hallowe'en is spooky.
Every Hallowe'en witches come out,
People dress up and go trick or treating.

Hallowe'en is great fun,
Some people have parties,
I like Hallowe'en night.
Sometimes it rains,
People dress up as witches and ghosts
And other things.

Mairead McShane (11)
St Rose's High School

Windows Of Life

Windows are the lens of life,
From my window the world is clear.
People come and people go,
No one realising I am here.

I see the lives of rich and poor,
I hear the cries, I hear the laughs.
The fun the love, the hatred and the joy,
I see all from one small pane.

Gillian Armstrong (15)
Strathearn School

THE TRAIN

Everything speeding by my window,
Nothing seems to stop.
Branches and twigs hit my window
But, does the train stop?

No, it keeps on running,
Running from the trees,
Right out to the seaside
To the salty breeze.

Nobody can stop it
As the train whizzes by,
Until it gets to the station
To pick up more allies.

As the station master blows his whistle
Now, we're off again,
Right out to Africa
To the desert plain.

Now sand hits my window,
I cannot see.
Sand, sand everywhere,
Just the desert and me.

Now we're off to the jungle
To meet our monkey friends,
They are waiting for us
At the river's bend.

Now we're getting sleepier,
Though the train carries on.
Tomorrow the journey starts again,
When we visit China, Hong Kong.

Helen Bell (13)
Strathearn School

My Two Windows

Outside my two windows
Is the world that I live in.
When I look through them the world is clear,
But when I don't, my vision dissolves.

I am told to be revolting and disgusting
Whenever I look through them.
I feel as if they defied me,
As I cry myself to sleep.

My barrier against the usual blurry world
Is smashed, for it protects me no more.
They made me angry, but I made a decision
To try to see through them once more.

It's been well over a decade now
And I'm happy to the core.
My vision is clear, and I'm not 'ugly' now,
And that's because . . .
I don't need my glasses any more!

Nadine Norwood
Strathearn School

Window Of The Soul

Windows of the soul
Tell a story in every eye,
A lie in every movement
And a thought in every blink.

Windows of the soul
Transparently they show
More sensitive the touch,
The deeper each one goes.

A window of the soul
Can never be misread,
The clearer the window
The more there is to know.

Ruth Osborne (16)
Strathearn School

THE THINGS I HATE MOST!

T he sound of the teachers moaning,
H elp me they never stop groaning!
E arly in the morning.

T his day is going to be so boring.
H urry up or we'll be late!
I hurried through the school gate.
N o one there in sight
G oodness I don't feel too right!
S huffling and struggling I have to get to class.

I 'm finally here - at last!

H orrid people make me feel sad
A nd most of all, they make me feel bad.
T urnips and cauliflower I hate too.
E ven broccoli and most of all mange-tout.

M aybe I'll like them when I grow older,
O h Mum, that's rubbish, I told her.
S o there you go, that's my story,
T he only thing is - I hope it wasn't too boring!

Emma Cranstone (12)
Strathearn School

PERFECT WINDOWS

The perfect summer window
Has the perfect view I create in my mind.
The sun is shining bright and people are smiling.
The people talk and laugh with no one left behind.

The perfect autumn window
Has the perfect view I create in my mind.
Crispy orange leaves flying through the air,
All the ladies' hair blowing in the wind.

The perfect winter window
Has the perfect view I create in my mind.
Ice-white snowflakes fluttering to the ground.
A snowball hits you in the face for a second you think
                                    you've gone blind.

The perfect spring window
Has the perfect view I create in my mind.
Baby lambs skipping across the field,
Daffodils being picked by someone very kind.

Pauline Twibill (15)
Strathearn School

LOVE

Physically challenging,
Heart-wrenchingly painful
Timeless pauses
Never-ending thoughts.

Each moment different,
With some kind of hidden fear.
Will the end bring death,
Or a lifetime of sadness.

For some people this,
The most complex, divided
Mixed emotion,
Only come once in a heart-shaped moon,
Love.

Sarah McMinn (15)
Strathearn School

YOUNG AND OLD WINDOWS

I sit here, looking out of the window to my future.
The sun sparkles shimmering light through my window,
As I wonder about all the opportunities that may come
Of how many different people I will meet
And of all the people I'll never know.
Where will the different paths lead me,
And will I always choose the right one?
Of all the choices that there are to be chosen,
So much is unknown.

I sit here looking out of the window to my past,
The dim light fades into darkness.
As I wonder about all that I have left behind,
About all the people who I could have known,
Of all the different paths that I came along,
Of all that is left for me now,
As I have no choice,
But to sit here and wonder about what could have been,
And about what I could and should have done.
I know it all now, nothing is unknown.

Andrea Leebody (15)
Strathearn School

Looking Through My Window

As I look through my window,
My world freezes in time.
People outside walk on by,
Trying to drag their screaming child.

I sit there for hours
And watch their world go by.
It's cold and lonely outside,
Despite all the festive designs.

In my world, it's warm,
And cosy, no festive designs in here.
Just my dog and me,
Looking through my window.

Watching their world go by
In the blink of an eye.

Stephanie MacNeill (15)
Strathearn School

Fifteen Years To Go

I sit alone in the darkness,
just wall and bars separating me from the outside world.
Looking out I can see the sun
shining on the girl with the dog
and the man cruising in his new car,
but not on me.
For those on the outside, the sun is always shining,
For me, on the inside, it rains.

I sit alone in the darkness
just another fifteen years to go,
watching lives pass me by,
watching my life pass me by,
just sitting, alone in the darkness.

Vicky Bill (14)
Strathearn School

THE ESOTERIC LAKE

That lake in the forest will always puzzle me,
I visited it one day with great mystery.
I could see myself in it, forest and all
But no sound came from it, not even a call.
I couldn't see in what was below was a secret,
I stared at it, it stared back
I couldn't help feeling something was trapped.
As if they couldn't get out and I couldn't get in,
And that sheet of glass was its prison.
I wondered about it, was it a he or a she?
I am nearly sure it was thinking of me.
I couldn't see it, but its knowledge was there,
As if I wasn't the first to wonder and stare.
I wanted to help, but I didn't know how,
I couldn't do anything but wrinkle my brow.
I wanted to stay, but I had to go now
It seemed to understand, I'm not quite sure how.
I left the lake feeling sad and dismayed,
Wondering how many more lakes happened to be in this way.

Susan Moore (15)
Strathearn School

My Window

As I unwrap my Christmas presents and laugh with my family,
I look out of the window to catch a glimpse of a dark figure.
I wonder why this dark figure isn't at home with its family,
Because after all, Christmas is a family time.

All of a sudden, things start spinning round and round.
I find myself on the other side of the window now.
I am that dark figure wandering the dark and quiet streets,
And I am the person without a family or friends.

If only it was me who was on the warm side of the window,
And if only I had a family or friends to spend Christmas with,
Then I would no longer have to create what my life would be,
If I was the person on the bright side of the window.

Danielle Futter (14)
Strathearn School

Windows

I'm looking through a world of knowledge.
At the touch of a button, I can be anywhere,
Talking to anyone.
I'm looking through a world of opportunity,
There are so many ways to surf the net.
It feels slow to type a word,
But I know my voice is heard.

Julia Bailey (11)
Strathearn School

DIRTY BIRD

Stain on my window,
Dirty bird,
Trying to clean,
Not wanting to touch,
The sponge is filthy,
The window is dirty.

Another stroke of soapy water,
The window sparkles
It glistens in the light,
Until two days later,
My curtains opened,
To find another stain,
My window will only stay clean,
When all the dirty birds die.

Laura Matthews (15)
Strathearn School

WINDOWS

As I gaze through the window on a lovely summer's day,
I notice the birds are chirpy and gay.
I see the beach and hear children scream
Asking their parents for a nice, cold ice-cream!
Then as the sun falls slowly from the darkened sky,
The birds stop chirping and sing a lullaby,
I wonder why,
I wonder why the sun has slowly said goodbye?

Chantelle Derrick (11)
Strathearn School

FROM THE OTHER SIDE OF THE WINDOW

The poor beggar stared in the window
At the happy family inside,
He felt like his heart was broken
But from whom should his tears hide?

His tears slid down his grubby face
And splashed into the puddles on the ground
He wiped them away with his torn sleeve
And left without a sound.

Night began to fall,
Once again he felt alone,
He wished that he had a window,
Some furniture, a family, a home.

All he wanted was a window
From which he could stare,
To hear the rain splash off
But from that he was bare.

He hoped when he was older
That he'd live in an old people's home,
So he could stare out of the window all day long,
And never again be alone.

Louise Rodgers (12)
Strathearn School

LOOKING IN

As I look inside the window here,
I see a feast. It's all so clear.
I wish it was me in there
Eating the feast, beside the fire.

People dancing and singing,
All enjoying themselves.
There is me,
The man outside the window,
Seeing everything so clear.

Nicola Keenan (11)
Strathearn School

THE LAST LESSON OF THE DAY

It's the last lesson of the day
And I'm almost bored to tears,
But never fret or worry,
Three-thirty is nearly here.

I look through the open window
As the sun beams down,
The drone of the teacher's voice
In the background.

I dream of being out there,
Free to do what I please,
The heat of the sun
And the coolness of the breeze.

I hear the dogs bark
And the birds in the trees sing,
But my only hope is
For the bell to ring.

The trees are starting to sway now,
Where the birds once sang,
But who cares anyway,
The bell just rang!

Claire Cooper (15)
Strathearn School

Memory Windows

I was looking out of the window
(There were about two minutes to go)
The wind was blowing wild in the trees,
I'm thinking of them, are they of me?

Day dreaming about old Strandtown School
Of the eleven plus, friends I knew
Allison, Rachael, Deborah, Heather,
Frost on the window, winter weather.

As the rain came on, the feeling passed,
The teacher's voice brought me back to class
And as I turned round, what did I see?
Everyone was the same as me!

Holly Martin (11)
Strathearn School

Summer Outside My Window

I wake up,
The window is open,
I can hear the hubble-bubble of the street below.
I open my curtains and sneak a peek outside.
The sun is splitting the trees,
The sky is blue, without a cloud in sight.
A bird sits on the sill and sings sweet summer tunes,
Kids are out in the street playing.
Old Mr Taylor is washing his car,
Mrs Grimes is taking her dog for a walk.
I can't wait to be out there,
Looking in at everyone who is missing all the fun.

Christine Millar (15)
Strathearn School

WINDOWS - WHICH ONE DO YOU LIKE?

Circular, rectangular, square and round,
which one to you makes the sound?

Are they smiling, laughing or frowning at you,
do you know? I don't think you do!

Or do you prefer the type that are fun,
magical, imagine a singing computer one?

The dancing, prancing joyful thing
I can do almost anything,
I can type, I can draw, you must agree
it's the best one to see!

Megan Thompson (11)
Strathearn School

ADVICE FROM STONE

Looking out through the window of life,
I feel pity for those struggling in strife.
As they hurry along at an uncomfortable pace,
They all compete in an imaginary race.
If only I could speak, I would try to slow them down,
Remind them life's too short to be running all the time,
But as I stay in my position,
No one gives me recognition.

After all, I am only a statue.

Ruth Caven (15)
Strathearn School

WINDOWS

Walking home on a December day,
Many windows along the way,
Showing me glimpses of other lives,
Happy children, busy wives.

Trudging in the slushy snow
Through the window is the glow
Of a Christmas tree, so pretty and bright,
Flooding the dreary garden with light.

In another, a frail old lady sits,
Patiently she waits and knits.
Will someone visit her at home,
Or must she sit and wait alone?

At my home without a doubt,
My pet dog will have his snout
Pressed up against the windowpane,
Waiting to greet me once again.

Katherine Dalzell (15)
Strathearn School

FLYING WINDOWS

Staring through the window
Watching cars go by,
My imagination takes me
I don't know where,
I don't know why.

Flying over rooftops,
Higher than a cloud
Watching people down below
Walking, talking, laughing out loud.

When suddenly I'm on the bed,
Lying half asleep,
With my mum shouting up to me,
Saying, 'Heather, time for tea.'

Heather MacNeill (11)
Strathearn School

CHILDREN AND WINDOWS

The children look through the window
Longing for the rain to stop,
To play in it once again.

In the garden playing football,
They kick it high,
Smash goes the window
As the ball goes right through it.

In a car on a long journey,
The children gazing out of the window,
Wondering when they will finally arrive.

Children run to the window
To peer out,
When they hear someone is coming up the drive.

As you walk down the street
And you look in a window,
You know a child lives there
When there are toys on the window sill.

The children bored,
Half an hour before home time
They look through the window,
Longing for home time to come.

Sarah Meadows (13)
Strathearn School

THE CHANGE

I open the window and look around,
I study the clouds not making a sound,
Each one different in their own special way,
Looking around as the sun fades away.

Each ray bounces off the glass
As I watch each one of them pass,
They make a glint with a colourless tint.

The sun hides behind the hilly plain,
My concentration starts to wane
Until the window starts to change,
To colours far beyond my range
Orange, lilac, silver, blue,
The sunset changed the old glass to new.

Laura Nixon (14)
Strathearn School

A WINDOW

As I fondly gaze out of the cheery bright window,
A flash of light comes thundering in,
Like an army of many soldiers,
A ray of light and following colours come in like the major
                                                         and his troops,
As they come in they line up, lying long and straight.
There is ruby red and emerald green and many more are
                                                         parading in,
There is a loud noise, a thundering kind of what I cannot tell,
But sooner than they came in, they were gone again.

Ruth-Anne Wilgar (13)
Strathearn School

MY KALEIDOSCOPE WINDOW

The church, so silent, solemn, dark and dull
Is lit up by the beautiful
Magnificent windows.
Stained glass, many colours and designs, scarlet, emerald,
                                        sapphire, ruby red
Even more above my head.
Candles flicker and glitter against the window, which
                                    twinkle and glimmer
With the moonlight
Beaming onto the glass,
Making a rainbow of impressions on the opposite walls
And along the halls of the church.

Kathryn Duff (13)
Strathearn School

OUTSIDE THE WINDOW

Looking through my bedroom window I can see
small children jumping in puddles and squealing with glee.
The black Labrador is barking with joy,
I can hear the squeaking from its little rubber toy.
The noise dies down as the children go in,
the black Labrador is running in too,
no one is left in the street and the trees have stopped sighing.
All that is left is the pitter-patter of the rain.

Emma Campbell (11)
Strathearn School

Windows Of Opportunity

I wonder what will happen to me,
Twenty years from now,
Will I be a millionaire in a mansion,
A commoner with a house,
Or a poor person with nothing?
It depends if I get opportunities
And spend my money wisely.
I wonder if I wish, will the windows open for me?
I hope the windows will open
To take care of my career, children and luck.
Oh I wish so!
I wonder if my wondering and wishing
Has opened the windows for me?
As I stare at the sky, long after night has settled.

Jennifer Stewart (11)
Strathearn School

When I Look Out Of The Window

When I look out of the window,
Up at the clear blue sky,
I can see butterflies flapping their wings gracefully,
And children playing around the flower beds,
Where the bees come and go,
And when rain falls,
It gently splashes on the leaves of the old oak tree . . .
When I look out of the window.

Katie Bill (11)
Strathearn School

Looking Through The Window

The sapphire sky up above
Makes me think of birds in love,
Grey sky catches my eye,
Makes me think of people who have died.
Children outside playing in the street,
Running and jumping on their little feet,
Gazing and peering is what I like to do,
Thinking I'd like to be out there too.
The sun shines brightly in that sapphire sky,
That's what I like to see,
I like to see the bumblebee
Fly right into a flower,
And watch until it comes out again,
Buzzing as loud as they are.
Then it pours and I suddenly feel dull,
Ideas are going out of my skull,
The rain pours down,
Pitter-patter, pitter-patter,
Night has just begun.
Night has fallen and the sky has gone black,
I'm really tired and I'm going to fall back,
Back into a world of gaze,
The stars are so bright,
They practically blaze,
It's time to fall asleep again,
Into a world that's totally insane.

Katherine Best (11)
Strathearn School

GRAVEYARDS

I look through my window
Into the graveyard,
There is only one tiny corner
That is beaming with light.

Its colours are beautiful,
The birds are singing,
The flowers are blooming,
The trees are alive.

Now everything is dying
And the sky is turning black,
Sadness is dawning
And memories are coming back.

I can only see all evil,
As the clouds close off the sky,
The trees and flowers are withering
And the graveyard is now gone.

Emma Thompson (13)
Strathearn School

THE WORLD THROUGH A WINDOW

The world flies by in an instant second,
Right before my eyes.
It's amazing what you an see
Through a window of this size.

The world is spinning outside this window,
Allowing me to see,
Each and every car and building,
All the plants and trees.

But within a few more seconds,
The world it stops, stands still.
As I watch, some others join me
By the train seat window sill.

Emily Wyeth (13)
Strathearn School

WINDOW OF DARKNESS

As I stared through the window
Of dark anxiety,
Hatred possessed my soul.

I strode along and held my ground
Firm beneath my feet,
Winning was my goal.

For many years I'd hidden away,
Kept to myself
But now I was back and strong.

I'd been pushed aside then,
But not anymore,
I would show them they were wrong.

I stood there bravely
And fought a battle of words,
Until finally they let me pass.

At once my window was shattered,
Bright light glowed into my life,
And all that was left of my past
Was splintered, broken glass.

Faye Caldwell (13)
Strathearn School

Fairy Out Of The Window

As I peered out of my window,
I got a nice sight,
A magical fairy
Flying at night.

Against the black night sky,
She glittered so bright,
Brighter than any star that night.

With long blonde hair and two purple wings,
This little fairy began to sing,
It was something I had never heard,
And nothing else could be compared.

What I saw out of my window
That magical night
Will always be a memory
For the rest of my life.

Julie Hedley (14)
Strathearn School

The Porthole

When I look through the porthole, what do I see?
A big wide ocean of blue and green,
All around me the waves are crashing
And on the porthole, the rain is lashing.

When I look through the porthole, what do I see?
A big wide ocean of blue and green,
Boats are bobbing up and down
And seagulls are flying all around.

When I look through the porthole, what do I see?
A big wide ocean of blue and green.
The fish are swimming all around,
They are making not a sound.

When I look through the porthole, what do I see?
A big wide ocean of blue and green.
All around me the waves are crashing
And on the porthole the rain is lashing.

Elaine Clarke (13)
Strathearn School

COLOURS THROUGH A WINDOW

Looking through the shop window at the sight before my eyes,
All the bright colours shining as each one lights up the sky.
A work of art displayed before me, scarlet, purple, gold and blue,
Without bright colours in the world, what on earth would we do?

Colours are used every single day, for colours on paper, lots of money we pay,
From looking at objects to describing our clothes,
Bright colours are even painted on our tiny little toes.
People don't realise just how important colours are.

From bright colours to dull ones is like changing from happy to sad,
living in a world with colours makes me proud I have to add.

So to conclude, I'd like you to think of the people stuck indoors,
Without windows, colours would be lost for them,
Their world would be dull. Oh what a shame!

Ashley Porter (14)
Strathearn School

My Window, My Journey

As I look from my window, the scenery passing by,
I can't see a thing, it's flashing before my eyes.

The animals awaking from their slumber as on my journey
I cans see the glorious things fly by.
I can see birds, I can see trees,
I'm glad I've got windows. Oh, look at the bees.

Well I've been on my journey and world has turned dark.
Now I can see from my window the moon, the stars, the pitch
black sky,
The trees have disappeared, oh please tell me why?
The life outside has died now and everything is asleep,
The scenes I've seen from my window are memories that I'll keep.

Gillian Brown (13)
Strathearn School

The Window

I look out of the window and I see the adults and children.
In the world around me
I see trees being blown in the wind, the sun shining through
the thick rain clouds,
I see children playing outside with their friends, and adults rushing
to get to work,
I could hear cars and buses taking people to work
And people talking as they walk past.

Amy McLaughlin (13)
Strathearn School

A Window Of Opportunity

A window is a looking glass,
Mirroring trees and emerald grass.
Through a window you can see
A branch of leaves swaying helplessly.

A window is a looking glass,
For whatever world you choose to see,
It may be bright and rich and full,
Or it could be dull and cloudy.
But for whichever world you choose to see,
My world is bright and cloud free.

A window is a looking glass,
A two-way portal for all who pass,
To glimpse a world not your own,
Be it with your friends or all alone.

Jennifer Cash (14)
Strathearn School

Looking At The Storm

The sky was dark above the sea,
The waves were rumbling, wild and free.
Rain was tapping on the ground
Making such an awful sound.
As I looked out of the window that terrible day
Thunder was coming from far away,
The boat was rocking on the sea,
Rain was pouring in front of me.
The storm gave a final warning sign,
At last the sun began to shine.

Katie Higgins (12)
Strathearn School

DIFFERENT WINDOWS

Stained glass windows
Gleaming and bold,
Reflecting colours on the floor
Like a motionless kaleidoscope.

Windows in an old shop
Streaked with dirt and neglected.
Scratched, rough woodwork
Frames the rectangular eyesore.
The owner of the shop has long gone home;
The windows are empty and all alone.

New windows in a house
Reflect images, almost mirror-like.
Clean and shiny,
With pearl-white plastic frame.
Lit up, criss-crossed with lead
Like strange eyes in the night when everyone's in bed.

Gemma Scott (14)
Strathearn School

THE SECRET WORLD

I looked into the window
And saw a different world,
The tiny people living there
Were very unperturbed.

I don't think they saw me,
Or heard me move around,
To see what they were doing
In their world so free of sound.

In the end, I just got bored
Of creeping like a mouse,
I looked again through the window
At this silent, still dolls' house.

Claire Kirker (14)
Strathearn School

WINDOW OF DREAMS

In that beautiful, big house,
A red and orange hearth is blazing.
The best china is placed out,
Full of delicious food.

I look down at my own clay bowl,
Empty.
I see my cold, blue hands.
O to warm them over that blazing hearth.

As they get up,
Someone proposes a toast,
And then they dance,
In all their fine clothes.

I stand up
And in my dazzling gown,
I dance with a handsome prince.
I curtsey,
Everyone applauds,
Then I am back in reality again.

Rachel Manning (12)
Strathearn School

The Window

The window protects us from the freezes,
Keeping us warm through winter breezes.
On sunny days the room is bright,
The glass lets through loads of light.
On rainy days the rain keeps out,
Charging like bullets, but none make it, nought.
Through bleak grey storms the glass stays intact,
No matter how morbid we feel the day is, in fact.
On windy days I can hear the window whining,
While as if in competition the wind is howling.
Still the windowpane survives the rages,
Holding up through all the ages,
Until suddenly one day a football came flying,
And with an amazing smash, all in a flash, the windowpane was dying.
Oh what a window pain!

Caroline Bole (13)
Strathearn School

Windows

Through the window,
the orange sun is shining in the bright blue sky,
the sparrows sitting twittering in the tree so high,
children running shrieking in and out of the trees,
the slow and gentle humming of the summer bees.
Babies splashing in the pools, laughing and sometimes crying,
the low swooping of their wings as the geese are flying.
Silent is the dog, sleeping in the sun
everyone happy and doing their own thing,
having so much fun.

Florence Andrew (11)
Strathearn School

LOOKING THROUGH A PORTHOLE

On a ship, drifting away from the
Land to the sea,
Looking out of a porthole at the
Lonely, blue sky,
A seagull flies by.

On a cruise liner, the sun rising on
The horizon,
Everybody sleeping, not me,
Through a porthole, I see the sun glowing,
Red, orange and yellow.

Y is for yacht, a rowing boat with
A sail
In the cabins, looking out of a porthole,
I hear the adults laughing above,
The fish swimming down below.

Fishing boats catching fish,
Out of a porthole I see fishing nets
And lobster cages,
Wet decks of boats as fish slip around,
Fish caught as I watch out of a porthole.

Joanne McKeown (11)
Strathearn School

OLE BILLY

Ole Billy was a cowboy of the finest class,
He rounded steers and then went home to supper with his lass.

He had a horse of dapple grey, the finest in the West,
And of all the cowboys' cabins, Billy had the best.

But Billy wasn't satisfied, 'cos Billy had a dream,
He wanted to be Sheriff and catch Big Mickey Mean.

Mickey was a bandit, feared throughout the land
And long ago he robbed our Billy, of his own right hand!

Our Billy wasn't one to forgive and then forget,
He knew it was no accident, he'd get Big Mickey yet!

So although Billy grieved when the Sheriff passed away
He knew what it meant, it meant his lucky day.

He became the County Sheriff, a most respected man
And sitting in his office, Billy made his plan.

On a hot day in July, he heard a whistle sound,
He saw it was a goods train and asked where it was bound.

So Billy and his deputy and band of merry men
Leapt aboard the train, at the luggage end.

He knew that Mickey Mean would stop the loaded train
Unable to resist the baccy and the grain.

The cowards in the cabin would obey his every word,
But Billy and his men were waiting there, unheard.

Everything that happened went according to the plan,
And Mickey went to jail, minus his right hand!

But over the years the legend it grew,
Till now it is a tall tale, very untrue.

That Billy fought Big Mickey, single-handedly
And no one knows the truth, 'cept for you and me.

But still it has a moral to lead an honest life
And not to touch no hands with no sharpish knife!

Claire Thompson (12)
Strathearn School

WINDOWS

Driving through the lonesome city,
I see squares of glass shimmering,
Some lit up by bright light,
But few with flickering candlelight.

Most dark and gloomy like their city,
Shadows here and there, silhouettes of figures,
Some shying away from the world,
With blinds or protective curtains.
I gaze through the window of the bus
Wondering what there is to look at.
I see the shadows of my eyes,
Scared and alone, wondering will this bus ever stop?

So few people aboard, also silent,
Looking dismayed at their window.
The large windows now being covered
In small droplets, gradually beginning
To take over the window.
Now everything is a blur,
I cannot see anything clearly,
But then again, what is there to see?

Elizabeth Bree (15)
Strathearn School

PRECIOUS IMAGES

As I stare out through my bedroom window, and look out
at the world. The view that I get is spectacular.

I see the colours of the rainbow in everything that I see
as the light flashes by, like electrifying lightning.

Emeralds and rubies with specks of gold rush past as I
look at my reflection and realise that I am growing old.

The radiant sunlight projects the images of the busy world down below.

Without my window I would have no light, no hope, no confidence.

To see what is coming my way, and what to expect is a
special gift to be treasured.

Rachelle Thompson (14)
Strathearn School

THE PLANE

Warm and content up high in the sky,
a blur outside the window as the world passes by.
Moving so fast, at the speed of light,
after a while, day turns to night.
Lightning begins to appear as a storm draws near,
passengers on the plane look out in fear,
feel the sweat on my hand,
I hope that safely the plane will land.

Jacci McLellan (16)
Strathearn School

THE WINDOW

Life through a window
Is all she has.
Never been out in the *Big World,*
She gazes at the flashes of
Green, red, blue and yellow, as
The people hurry by.

She wonders what it's like
To be out hurrying with the other people.
Then she thinks to herself, it
Couldn't be right. She is safe and warm
In her glowing house, with her parents standing by,
And wonders how she could ever think
Of being outside.

For the people are cold hearted
And never have the time
To talk, laugh; say hello or even say goodbye.
This girl is an invalid, who will
Probably never see the outside world.

Life through a window
Is all she has.
Never been out in the *Big World,*
She contentedly turns away
From the insecurity of outside, to
The security of her home.

Jennylee Cooling (14)
Strathearn School

A Winter Window Scene

I sit in the black velvet window seat
And watch the people below pass by.
Their movements looking like ants
On this cold, windy December day.

Above me the sky is a coloured
Smoky quartz crystal,
Below, the pearly snow-covered streets
Slowly turn to mush.
On the windowpanes an
Ivory frost appears
Above the ebony window sill.

The sky opens and fluffy flakes fall,
The streets become smothered by snow.
The view from the window is blinded,
This thin pane of glass is all
That separates me from the elements.

Gemma McGuire (16)
Strathearn School

Windows

As I walk down the long, dark street,
Snow falling, covering my feet,
I think to myself what is life about
As I see people in the window looking out.

Through the window is a family together,
Probably thinking they will be like that forever,
But then again, I once thought the same way
'Cause everything changes I must sadly say.

The window was filled with happiness and joy,
As the baby played with his brand new toy,
Watching this truly helps me to see
How much my family means to me.

Long windows, short windows, round and square,
It's started to rain, that's really not fair.
The view through the windows is no more,
Until the sun shines and brings colours galore.

Jenna Fielding (15)
Strathearn School

THE CHURCH WINDOW

Bright colours with sunlight shining through,
Nothing lost in shadow,
Vivid colours paint a pattern on the tiled floor below,
Splinters of light flicker all around.
The world outside is forgotten, fear and sorrow drowned
When the sunlight shines twinkling beams project.
Though not transparent, the window shows a world of colour
And bright shining images,
Like a mirror, it reflects rich shades at angles,
But once light fades
The nave is left in darkness.
The warmth and strength of light has faded
All is forgotten
Light stains the floor no more.
Now still and silent,
The lonely church
Awaits the dawn.

Rachel Grimes (14)
Strathearn School

LIFE IS A WINDOW

The window of life is open,
Open to all,
But not all grab it with both hands
And appreciate what they have.

When born to the world, one is naïve.
The years pass by, lessons are learned.
You become independent,
An independent window.

The frame is strong and sturdy,
It is the basis of every soul.
Some draw blinds for protection,
For resistance against the world.

The pane gives opportunity.
It is through the glass
That light streams
To illuminate your life.

In life, windows open,
Windows close,
Windows shatter.

Laura Wilson (16)
Strathearn School

STEEL BARS

Steel bars form the window of the prisoner's cell,
dull and dark they lock away a criminal.
He looks out every day at the dark clouds that lurk
over head, and remembers his life outside.
He clasps the bars with his hands and shakes with all
his strength, but as before they do not move and he is
stuck inside for another day,
of his miserable seven year sentence.
Without the window he would go mad,
he would look at the walls, boring and grey;
but now he can look through the gaps in the steel bars
and watch the world slide by.

Rachel Boyd (14)
Strathearn School

LIGHTNING OUTSIDE THE WINDOW

As lightning strikes this dark grey sky,
Gold flashes flicker in my eye,
All the birds that flew up above
Take shelter with the ones they love.
The thunder roars,
The wind soars,
The streets seem dead,
Thoughts are leaving my head.
Will this storm end, or shall I pretend?

Jamielee Bingham (11)
Strathearn School

MEMORIES OF A SPACE FLIGHT

In the blackness I floated
Tumbled and turned, over and over
No more pain or hate or fear
Everything was simple then
Me against the universe
I could see the earth far, far below me
And see the stars surrounding and dazzling me
I saw the moon and the bright, hot sun
And saw a star whose life had just begun
I saw a spacecraft explore and learn
And how one life can change the world.

Rachael O'Flaherty (15)
Strathearn School

THE MILLENNIUM

On New Years Eve
There's a big party in town,
So don't be sad and don't give me a frown
Grove to the music
And listen to the beat
And let's all move and shuffle our feet.
The clocks strikes twelve
The New Year is here
So let's all party and drink our beer.

Wendy McCallin (13)
Victoria College

OUR STREET AT NIGHT

Night time falls over our street,
Lights shine out of house windows,
Onto the black tarmac road.
Teenagers walk up to the shop and back again,
Talking and shouting as they walk.
Mr B sleeps in his living room,
Probably snoring with every breath he takes.
The boys are playing hide and seek,
Shrieking when they find each other.
Tina barks without stopping,
Every time something moves.
My sister and her friend
Push prams around the street, chattering away.
Matthew K runs home to go to bed,
Shouting that he doesn't want to.
Mr Mc rides home on his motorbike,
But first stops to talk to my dad.
Mr G drives home,
In his noisy sports car.
All the cats stalk around
Looking for scraps to eat.
All the boys
Run into their houses.
My sister says goodbye
To her friend
Before going into the house.
Tina stops barking
And crawls into her kennel.
The street is silent
As everything falls asleep.

Laura Martin (11)
Victoria College

CHRISTMAS!

On Christmas Day
The children play
And all the girls and boys
Bring out their toys
That Father Christmas brought them.

They go outside
And make a slide
Of ice, snow and water.
When dinner time comes,
They run into the kitchen
To see the big chicken
Waiting for them to eat him.

After dinner, they exchange presents
And open them with lots of cheer
While the adults sit and drink beer
And have a good chit-chat about the year
But also say *Merry Christmas and a Happy New Year*!

Christine Sterrett (12)
Victoria College

MY GUINEA PIG

My guinea pig is black and white,
I'm sure she stays up half the night,
She loves to sleep and play on the grass,
My guinea pig she's really class!

My guinea pig lives in a big, spacious hutch
And lots of room is never too much,
I feed her vegetables for her lunch,
My guinea pig loves to nibble and munch.

My guinea pig's fur is very soft,
I wouldn't dare put her up in the loft,
She loves to run to drive me round the bend,
My guinea pig is my favourite furry friend.

Katie Burrell (11)
Victoria College

THE SCHOOL TRIP

The children, excited,
Bounce up and down on the bus,
But it's just a trip, what's all the fuss?

As the bus arrives at the museum,
The children begin their tactic game.
They crowd in through the small, opened doors,
'Stop!' the tour guide roars!

After destroying a T-Rex skull,
The children mutter, 'This trip
Is not too dull!'
The tour guide exhausted -
Collapses wearily,
And suddenly screams very loudly!
For the vainest girl in the class
Has just dropped a £10,000 looking glass!

'The Bus is here!'
The children and the *tour guide* cheer.
They shout goodbye to the museum,
We'll be back again - next year.

Amy Phillips (13)
Victoria College

LOVE, DEATH AND WAR

The war raged on and on and on and on
The man fought all day and night
The battlefield was full of death
The battlefield was full of fright.

A young woman came up to the man
Her face was filled with raging fear
As she fell to her knees
Blood rushing from her far and near.

The man noticed the face of his long lost love
The woman he left to go to the war
The woman he left that bore him a child
The woman he left all cold and sore.

He fell to the ground beside her face
He kissed her cold, cold lips
He wept and wept and then he paced
And said 'I love you to bits.'

As he raced to the nearest hospital
With the woman's body in his arms
The Nazis shot off his legs
The Nazis sounded the alarms.

He couldn't run no longer, his love was dead
He dropped her body on the floor
And trailed himself to safety
He lost too much blood and couldn't go
On any more.

He wished the other troops good luck
And slowly died through the pain
The other soldiers fought and fought
A victory to gain.

The ghosts of the woman and the man
Flew up to Heaven happy in love
The Nazis had lost, the English had won
The first poppy grew under a
Flying white dove.

Paula Lyons (14)
Victoria College

CHRISTMAS

Crackers have been popped all day
While all the children go out and play.

Hurry up and go to bed,
What's that noise, it's Santa's sled.

Reindeers with their nose so bright
Arrive with Santa in the night.

Imagine all the games we'll play
Because Santa is on his way.

Silver snowflakes falling hard
As you open your Christmas cards.

Trees going up with beads and bows
While we try to warm our toes.

Merry Christmas everyone
Don't be fighting just have fun.

Amazing Grace is what we sing,
Glory to the New Born King.

Singers go from door to door
Bringing joy to more and more.

Leann MaCaulay (11)
Victoria College

PEG

I'm in my bedroom trying to sleep,
But all I hear is creak, creak, creak.
I walk down my hall and stared,
At my mum's picture of Fred Astaire.

I decided to go and explore my attic,
So I took my gun so I could splat it.
I opened the door and felt a light breeze,
The dust in there made me sneeze.

As I blew my nose I heard
Someone knocking on the stairs.
As I turned around I saw
A shadow with a giant paw!

I followed the shadow down the stairs,
I looked down and all I see was hairs,
I felt this wet nose on my leg,
It turned out to be my pet dog Peg.

Jillian Reid (13)
Victoria College

PEACE

One night I had a dream,
No uniforms
Walking down the street.
No fighting,
No bombs,
No war,
Just peace and love.
But unfortunately, it was just a dream.

But I am the next generation
I won't follow in other people's footsteps.
I hope the world will change for the better,
Starting on the first of January,
The year 2000.

Janine McKnight (12)
Victoria College

HORSES

I love the way they toss their heads
And munch upon the hay
And prance about in muddy fields
Ready for the day.

I love the way they flick their tails
And nudge you with their nose
And canter to their hearts content
Or lie down for a dose.

I love the way they stamp their hoof
Impatient to get on.
They listen well to your commands,
They're supple and they're strong.

I love the way they look at you
With their great big glossy eyes
And the way they're unpredictable,
They could just buck or shy.

I love their lovely colours
Chestnut, roan and bay.
Their coats, they gleam like silver,
If you groom them every day.

Catherine Magee (11)
Victoria College

Who?

Who gives us such a fright?
And gives us work which takes all night?
Who screams and calls us lazy louts?
And gets cross because we scream and shout?
Who gives us very hard sums?
And makes us spit out our chewing gum?
Who teaches RE, maths and history?
And to us are quite a mystery?
Who gives us questions which are sometimes easy?
And works on a budget which is quite measly?
Who mainly acts crazy?
And at other times can be nice - amazingly.
Who is it that really is a human creature?
Well I'll tell you - it's my teacher!

Naomi Andrews (12)
Victoria College

The White Swan

The white swan flew high
Over yonder hills
Set against the sky
Surpassing all the mills.
So free, so true
A bird in flight
So white, so blue,
With all its might
The white swan flew high
Over yonder hills.

Stephney Girvan (13)
Victoria College

The Spooky Noise

I am in the kitchen and I hear a noise,
I get the knife at the poise,
I poke my head round the kitchen door,
Just to hear a faint roar.

Then my dog, Patch barks,
At the weird and strange sparks,
I go outside to calm him down,
Then I feel I have to frown,
At the strange little man across
The way from me,
Although it is hard to see I know . . .
He is a ghost!

Nicola Beattie (13)
Victoria College

Tiger

My cat's eyes are green and bright,
His coat is grey with hints of white.
I remember the time he used to chase
And in the grass he would prance with grace.
He really loves his time of play,
Although he sleeps for most of the day.
He's old now but he's still my friend,
I hope his life will never end.

Cathryn Crockett (12)
Victoria College

The Wacko Family

Down the valley, across the sea
Lives the Wacko family
In an island all alone
No electricity, not even a phone.

A boy called Daisy, a girl called Dan
Both live in this caravan
And their parents Des and Bree
That's the Wacko family.

Uncle Al and Auntie Jo
Often seem to come and go
For some odd reason they never stay
Not for more than half a day.

There is something wrong with the Wackos
They don't have fingers, they just have toes.
Their hair is dark, but often turns grey.
They go to work but don't get pay.

They might seem harmless, but do fear
They're very dangerous when they're near
Watch out in case they come near you
But it's a bit late now, cos I'm a Wacko too!

Kirsty Shawe (12)
Victoria College

MY DREAM

My dream is to work at the airport.
To see people off on long journeys.
To talk four different languages in one day.
To hear the sound of the propellers as they blow my tidy
                              hair into a scrambled egg mess.
To get people through the passport check,
To work overtime and be proud of it.

To eat airline food as a TV dinner on a Friday night.
To have to rush to get people on their planes on time.
To wear red shoes and red lipstick to look like a Barbie doll.
To have a hair net and look like I work at the
                           cheese counter at Tesco's.

Rachel Johnson (13)
Victoria College

FRIENDS

Friends are forever,
Friends never lie,
Friends will be with you till the day you die.
Friends are honest, friendly and kind,
If you make a new friend, the other friend won't mind.
Friends are the best.
They never leave your side
And if you're very lucky, you'll make a friend for life!

Carla Cochrane (11)
Victoria College

TEENAGE SHOPPING

On Saturday morning, my friends will call
We've money to spend, so we'll have a ball.
We're off to town, where there's shops galore
But where to start and which floor.
I see rows of CDs, through the windowpane
I'll buy my favourite, Shania Twain.
Into the changing rooms, but what to wear
We'll just try everything, even underwear.
Big tops, small tops, track suits, jeans
We love the fashion, us trendy teens.
Hunger sets in, we need a bite
So it's off to McDonald's, where the food is just right,
We eat and we chat, we laugh and we joke
As we finish our burger, our chips and our coke.
Then it's down to Castle Court, with Miss Selfridges next to Claire's
Bay Trading and H Samuels and the Gadget shop upstairs.
Now we're getting tired and our money's running low
The shopping day is over, so it's home we want to go.
It's a dash for the bus and we are nearly there
We just about made it, with no time to spare.
We sit back and rest, with our bags on our knees
Will we do it again next week? Oh! Yes please!

Kerry Floyd (14)
Victoria College

SUPERMARKET SWEEP IN 10 SECONDS FLAT!

Grab a trolley,
Here we go.
Let's go and shop
In Tesco.
Dairy first,
Milk and cheese,
Then we'll get the frozen peas.
Carrots, potatoes,
What else do we need?
We must shop at great speed!
Dog and cat food,
There's shampoo
And we'll take some corn flakes too.
Bacon, fish,
A chicken dish,
This trolley's getting heavish.
Pears and apples,
Melons, plums,
Now this trolley weighs a ton!
Lemonade
And orange squash.
'Are you sure we've enough dosh?'
Cakes and buns,
'Oh there's the bread!'
Now this trolley feels like lead!
One last thing,
Daddy's beer!
Let us go to the cashier.
Now let's go home.
Oops! We forgot the shaving foam!

Catherine Barbour (12)
Victoria College

CATS

Cats are furry, cats are neat,
Cats are dainty on their feet,
Cats crawl and creep and pounce,
Cats leap and jump and bounce,
Cats are hunters chasing mice,
Rats, birds or spiders entice,
Cats lap and lick and preen,
Not content until they're clean.
Clitter, clatter through the flap,
Up to bed, time for nap,
Hours and hours on the bed he lies,
Occasionally half opening his eyes,
He flicks his tail, mice in his dream,
His life is really quite supreme.

Helen De Ornellas (12)
Victoria College

CHRISTMAS IS A MAGICAL TIME

Christmas is when the lights shine bright
All the way through the night
Children are told to go to bed
Or he will not come as the legend said.
The towering Christmas tree,
Everyone is excited including me
It's a magical time of year
There will certainly be no tears.

On Christmas Day I get a toy
Thanks to that baby boy
The three Wise Men,
Melting snowmen,
Bright red berries
And a merry Christmas to you and all.

Christina Devenney (12)
Victoria College

HALLOWE'EN

Pointy hats,
Witches black cats,
Silent, swooping, whooshing bats.
Goblins and Ghouls
Scare the owls
Dancing around the bubbling,
Sizzling cauldron.

Showers of sparks
Light up the night
Twinkling stars
That shine so bright.

Trick or treat?
The children ask
Hiding their faces
Behind their masks
Hallowe'en
'It's here at last!'

Karen Nicholl (12)
Victoria College

TRICK OR TREAT

As I lie in my bed
I hear strange noises in my head
'Oooh' and 'Boo!' is what I hear
Being whispered in my ear.

I pull the covers above my head
'Come out, Rachel,' someone said
I looked up and saw my mum
'Some visitors have decided to come.'

I went downstairs and mum opened the door
I saw a teddy that said 'More.'
My mum gave him a massive sweet
Because he said, 'Trick or treat!'

Jade Adair (12)
Victoria College

HALLOWE'EN

Hallowe'en is coming and the witches are out
Yes! Yes! They're out and about
Have you ever seen a witch with a black cat?
Yes! Yes! He's really fat.
He has spooky green eyes and stays in disguise
While he's flying through the skies
Have you ever seen a ghost and did he say boo?
Have you ever seen a ghost and did he scare you?
Have you ever seen a bat hanging upside down?
Have you ever seen a bat wearing an extra large frown?
Have you ever seen a pumpkin with round gloomy eyes?
Yes! Yes! He's caught by surprise.

Sarah Dunlop (11)
Victoria College

THE GUIDE DOG!

He guides her where she needs to go,
He tells her when to say hello,
He helps her cross the road with care,
Whenever cars aren't passing there.
He goes and lifts the ringing phone
And in return he gets a bone.
He helps her to get into bed
Then he can rest his weary head.

Jennine Buchanan (12)
Victoria College

MY GRAN

I visit her every day in her little bungalow,
she's always cheerful and happy too and she is never low.
She's given me food galore
food, food, more and more,
Her wrinkles on her cheeks and glasses on her eyes,
She wears funny coloured clothes and never wears a tie,
her funny grin and her pointy little chin,
She tells me things about her past,
like short relationships that never did last,
about her school and games she played,
I like the things she tells me and all the things she says.

Keith Killops (14)
Wellington College

Poverty

Deep in darkest Africa
You will hear the cry
Of all the orphan children
Trying not to die.

Hunger is tradition
Food is a reward
Water is essential
Incurable disease.

Children have pot-bellies
They look at you in vain
They live like this
Through night and day
And even in the rain
People say it's a hard life
Living in this constant strife.

Dean Johnston (13)
Wellington College

Elephants

Enormous and grey as an old rugged cardigan,
They roar like a car engine on a winter's morning,
Then suddenly an almighty wave of the enormous finger,
Delicately lifting large amounts of grass off the floor.

They swash it about in their huge mouth
Calmly staring with a twinkling eye
At the people who pay to watch them.
They take life in a stride and walk with pride.

It brightens up the day of people whose feet ache,
Then they come to the fantastic beasts
To watch their skill at work
At the end of the day, they're glad to watch
The beasts at rest.

Rachel Gough (13)
Wellington College

PAST AND PRESENT

The sounds of sirens loud and strong,
The nights lonely, dark and long.
Streets are deserted, curfews now.
Time is serious, war's begun.

Men are fighting - shield and sword,
Horse to horse - back to back.
The sounds of their feet are mighty,
It's not the end . . .

Blood is poured like water from a tap.
The fear of death lies before them.
The sounds, the lights and everything flashes
In front of them,
The last cry, then death.

Some lie awake - waiting.
Waiting to be found, or waiting to rot.
Some remain with a pulse,
Alive to tell the tale.

A great victory is born . . .

Angela Shields (14)
Wellington College

The Dentist

While in the register room on the leather
Seats the squeaky venetian blinds.
With the table full of glossy magazines.
Waiting, waiting for the loud boom of the monsters voice.
As he sharpens his knives upstairs waiting to steal
Every tooth in your head to add to his collection.
Then it came but instead of the loud booming voice
It was low and quiet, my fear left my shivering spine
But doubled when I saw him.
He was much broader and taller with a sturdy back and a thick
Back like a rugby player.
I sat on the chair and as it lowered I felt more trapped
There was no turning back now.
The chair stopped
My lips were grasped and pulled open
He thrust every weapon in his arsenal into my mouth
I squermered and it was over, with a
Numb mouth and a new filling, it was over
All I could do was wait till next time.

Matthew Shearer (13)
Wellington College

Colours Of Autumn

September comes as summer ends
And with it autumn with its golden days.
Leaves fall as children play,
Screaming and shouting and feeling gay.

Autumn is the best of seasons
Rich in colours, full of cheer
Bright with gold and bronze and copper
Crowning glory of the year.

Autumn's feet are covered in a carpet of leaves.
Reds and yellows and greens
Autumn comes and autumn goes
Next comes winter and a blanket of snow.

Pamela Johnston (14)
Wellington College

ALIENS

Aliens can be green.
Aliens can be red.
Aliens can be mean.
They can zap you in the head!

Most are really quite weird.
Some are very like us.
Aliens eat jam donuts.
They even use the bus!

Aliens all come from planets,
In a big mad joint called Space.
If you take away their laser,
They will slap you in the face!

Aliens can be fat,
Aliens can be thin,
Aliens can be small enough,
To fit inside your bin!

Some aliens eat pies,
The kind that make them fly,
But if they fly too high,
They will surely die!

Ross Dunlop (14)
Wellington College

Lexicon

The dew of the morning grass
The succulent juices of a pear
The steel chains which are so rare
The id of intelligence
The whimsical sound of the hollow sky.

These are things I like,

The precipitation of our water vapoured voice
The luscious wet strawberries glistening in the light
The rusty iron gates which look so irreplaceable.
The impulse of running a race.

The humidity of steaming damp clothes,
The juicy liquid known as water
The scarce metal of coins
The quirk of winning.

These are the things I like,

The gyrate which we all go round but
Still come to the start
The saturated coat which lost its protection
The wail of knowing failure is upon you.
The uncanny thing known as nature,
The wharf where we used to go
The belligerent act of sibling rivalry
The warp of life.

These are the things I hate.

John Mooney (13)
Wellington College

MISERY

He arrived at the graveyard to be greeted by a gate
When pushed, it opened with a creak
He marched all the way to the peak
Trying not to make a sound
Knowing that his next move could be his last.

As he stood on the graveyard's mound
Covered in an eerie mist
He crept to the gravestones steadily
Trying not to awake the spirits
Or else it could be deadly.

From far away he could see the gravestones
Floating free above the town
The stars twinkled high above the sky
The graveyard towered over our town
Casting evil shadows from east to west.

A car screeched, a dog howled
All things to make your body jump out of its skin
Climbing closer to the graves through the clouds of mist
He couldn't believe it as he saw
The spirits arise from their graves.

As soon as he saw them rising
He knew he had to escape
To trip over a rock and fall to his death
Running and rushing he had to get free
I actually knew the boy, it was me!

Mark Burch (13)
Wellington College

GRANDA

He comes round every weekend without delay
He might take me anywhere, McDonald's or the bay.

He's reaching on eighty but still fighting fit
And he gets rather mad when he's called an old git.

I love the way he wears his hat, sloping to the side
I don't know what I'd do without him if he ever died.

His car's an old Fiesta, with rust from back to front
When he tries to start it gives an awful grunt.

His favourite sweets are spearmint Polos, he sucks 'em all day long
And if you bought him peppermint he'd tell you, you were wrong.

He always takes me to play pool, which is his favourite game
But if he ever beats me I never take the blame.

And so this is my final verse and he couldn't have done worse
So this poem I will think of when he's lying in the hearse.

Matthew Cranston (13)
Wellington College

THE EAGLE

Gliding through the sky with outstretched
Wings, swooping for its prey.
Taut wings rising with the thermals
To get higher and higher and fly away.

Sharp glinting eyes scanning the green
Mountainous carpet, ready to extend its
Talons and shred its prey. Opening its
Sharp long beak crying its call for meat.

Diving, turning and swirling at a victim
Soon to die, its brown, white and golden
Feathers shining in the light.
The talons dig in and blood leaks out.
The eagle has had a meal tonight.

Steven McClintock (13)
Wellington College

THE BELL

The bell with its rustic golden tinge
As the sun preys on it with its reflection
Though majestic as it seems is dumb and unaware.

Cast those hundreds of years ago
Has seen many events just come and go
Through lives lost and lovers found
But still is bound to its cobwebbed sanctuary.

Guards perch round it in the night
Cooing bravely but shivering with fright
But dawn brings light and dimly seen
The immense shadow slowly swings.

As the seasons have come and gone
Still it chimes its ancient song
Though people age and fade away
Still it's tone breaks the day.

Every night under a blanket of stars
Silent and still on the dew-washed grass
I watch the bell through its curving cast.

Christopher Deary (14)
Wellington College

BIRDS OF PREY

Elegantly flying in the sky
So high, so high,
These distinguished birds of prey
Often hunt throughout the day.

The eagle flying with wings so bright
The owl who only comes out at night
The osprey looking for its prey
It never causes any delay.

The falcon carrying at its feet
Another bird who suffered a defeat
These ravenous raptors eating flesh
All day eaters but the best.

The raptors are diurnal birds
Except the owl, how absurd
This raptor, night time hunter
Attacks you if you hunt her.

Elegantly flying through the sky
So high, so high,
These distinguished birds of prey
Often hunt throughout the day.

Thomas Allison (14)
Wellington College

MAYBE

Every country wears a mask
Our country wears a mask of violence
Of guns and bombs
It is a shade of funeral black.

Underneath is fields of crystal green
With flowers like rubies and emeralds or sapphire blue
We wonder what love is
We wonder all the time?

Is it butterflies in your stomach maybe?
Or kissing in the trees
Or is it fighting like little kids,
Is it? Maybe?

We say we hate each other
But is this not just love
We are all the little kids
We behave like them, don't we?

Maybe if we all grew up
Fighting might just vanish
Laughter would invade the streets
Maybe?

Sarah Smith (13)
Wellington College

THE WONDERS OF THE RIVER!

The ripples of the water
The crashing of the waves
The fish swimming happily
In the rock pools of the cave.

Further down the river
The waves become sinister
The fish hide in fright
All to be seen is the dark, lonely rocks.

The river comes to an end
As it rounds its last bend
Its estuary approaches
The cycle starts again!

Gillian Elder (13)
Wellington College

THE DELIGHT OF DOLPHINS

Gliding through the water,
smooth and flowing skin,
carefree and light-hearted,
They swim without a care.

Their hidden world of wonder,
must entertain their souls,
all day they glide with gaiety,
In their wonderland abyss.

The dolphins swim in spirit,
their sapphire downcast skin,
Their burning eyes delighted,
perceiving hidden worlds.

Julie Anderson (13)
Wellington College

THE WONDERS OF THE WAVES

My first aspect of the sea was on an immense rock,
Peaceful and blue,
The diminutive white smooth waves slowly arched over, and
Washing up the beach.
Abandoning swerving patterns on the sand.

Down off the rock I ran to the shingle beach
And down to the sea where the waves swirled round my feet,
Leaving white foam sticking to my trainers.
Then abandoning again, the sea left pebbles and shells behind, some
Dull and cracked, others shiny and smooth.

Explosive breakers crash against the cliffs pounding
And battering, waves form all was peaceful and blue,
All turned into aggression.

Robert Smyth (14)
Wellington College

FEELINGS OF THE FOREST

The forest enclosed me,
The smell of pine,
Sun on the leaves,
Fingers tracing the bark.
Shadows crawling, dancing,
Footprints
Or just mere imagination?
Logs heaped like mountains,
Air heavy, moist and warm.
Animals running,
Scampering noises.
Blue skies
White clouds like cotton buds
Fluffy, soft and light.
Buzzing bees,
Yellow black bombs, carrying honey.
Summer's here.
Fresh flowers, colours bright
Lying on the grass.
The waterfall crashed
On shattering rocks
Sending white droplets flying
Like a shower of sudden rain
Refreshing and cool.
A rain forest.

Victoria McAuley (13)
Wellington College